PRA*and* PROMISES *for a* Hurting World

LAURA FREUDIG

BARBOUR BOOKS
An Imprint of Barbour Publishing, Inc.

DEDICATION

To the many pastors and teachers I have had
the privilege of sitting under, whose careful
scholarship and faithfulness to God's Word
informs everything I write; and to my
husband, who watched the baby so I could.

ISBN 978-1-68322-774-8

Published by Barbour Books, an imprint of Barbour Publishing, Inc., 1810 Barbour Drive, Uhrichsville, Ohio 44683, www.barbourbooks.com

Our mission is to inspire the world with the life-changing message of the Bible.

Member of the
Evangelical Christian
Publishers Association

CONTENTS

INTRODUCTION

*W*hen I'm working in my garden, tending the soil is not at the top of my to-do list. I like to plant and weed and harvest, but beneath the tomatoes and cucumbers the soil has a life of its own. If I neglect it, my crops will suffer. Yields will fall off, and the plants that do grow will be stunted and fall prey to insects and disease. No amount of hoeing or pruning will secure a bountiful harvest in poor soil. Plants need rich, deep, fertile ground to flourish.

We too need rich soil—spiritual soil. But so often we think our spiritual soil is the world we live in, and we blame our stunted growth on the violence, despair, poverty, evil, and injustice around us. We think if circumstances were different, *we* would be different. But when we talk about producing the spiritual fruit God desires—love, joy, peace, patience, kindness, goodness, faithfulness, gentleness, and self-control—our fruitfulness is not dependent on circumstances. Our fruitfulness is about how closely we are grafted into Jesus Christ.

We *can* live faithful, fruitful lives in this crazy world because the rich soil we need is at the foot of the cross, and the vine we grow from is the person of Jesus Christ. In this book are scripture-rich, devotional-like prayers that can be used as meditations or prayer starters to enrich your quiet time and give you peace, comfort, and hope in this hurting world.

SECTION 1: *Love*

THE LAMB IS OUR LIGHT

*D*ear Father, the world seems dark to our eyes in these days. Sometimes it feels like it can't get any darker, but then it does. We hear about another earthquake, another mass shooting, another bombing. More innocent children are killed, more mothers will never again rock their babies, more fathers will never return home, more teenagers will never reach adulthood. Scores of others, Lord, will bears scars for the rest of their lives.

It's hard to live in this darkness, to have faith that light exists and is coming. But Your Word says we can bear fruit even when the world is dark because our light is the Lamb, Jesus, the Word Incarnate, who shines on us, in us, and through us. We pray for a flourishing visible to those around us that has no explanation apart from Your power in us. Not a flourishing of wealth and power, though; gold does not shine in the darkness. But Your love does. Give us Your love to light this dark world. Amen.

The city does not need the sun or the moon to shine on it, for the glory of God gives it light, and the Lamb is its lamp. The nations will walk by its light, and the kings of the earth will bring their splendor into it.
REVELATION 21:23–24 NIV

God Is Love

*L*ord, You are love. More than any other single word in the Bible, the word *love* describes You. It's so simple, but at the same time so mysterious, so beyond me. I am not love; loving is not my nature nor my habit. Sometimes I feel loved and sometimes I act lovingly, but my love is small, weak, and self-reflective. The difference between my love and Yours is like the difference between the moon and the sun. One simply reflects; the other is the source of all light. One is cold and pale; only the other can warm us.

But You offer Your love to me. You say if You, God, who *are* love, live in me, I will live in love. That shakes me! Thank You for these verses. Help me to meditate on them, knowing they were written for me. I acknowledge that Jesus is Your Son, and because of that He lives in me and I live in Him. I know and rely on the love You have for me. You are love. If I live in love, I live in You, and You live in me. Amen.

If anyone acknowledges that Jesus is the Son of God,
God lives in them and they in God. And so we know
and rely on the love God has for us. God is love.
Whoever lives in love lives in God, and God in them.
1 John 4:15–16 niv

Do You Hear What I Hear?

*D*ear Jesus, we are Your sheep, the people of Your pasture, loved and precious and *known*. Thank You for that pastoral metaphor, which is both humbling and comforting. For we are just like sheep: foolish, weak, small, and easily led astray. We are prone to wander; we feel it every day in the way our minds tend to things other than You. We are prone to complain with an irritating repetition and a blindness to the blessings around us. Hours or even days go by without us pricking our ears to the sound of Your voice, without looking up to see where we are in relation to where You are. And when we find ourselves in a predicament—far from home, far from the flock, far from You—we cry out and You are there.

But, Lord, we want to be able to feed Your sheep too, just like You commanded Peter to do. We don't want to be so continually lost that we're no help to the other lost sheep around us. Help us to persistently reorient our minds on You and Your loving voice, and keep our wooly ears open to the cries of others. Amen.

Peter was grieved because he said unto him the third time, Lovest thou me? And he said unto him, Lord, thou knowest all things; thou knowest that I love thee. Jesus saith unto him, Feed my sheep.
JOHN 21:17 KJV

Who Tells Me Who I Am?

*D*ear Lord and Father, You had me in Your mind from before the moment of my conception. You knew me before I drew my first breath. You caused every cell to divide, every bone to stretch and grow, every diverse piece to knit to every other as I was being formed. You are my Creator, and I belong to You. I am unique in all Your creation, and I am precious to You.

I find it so hard to remember this truth. Voices, words, and images that tell me otherwise bombard me daily. The voices and words tell me I'm missing, imperfect, wanting, less than, not enough. And when I compare myself to the images I see, I am shockingly flawed. Lord, I want Your voice to drown out all others. I want Your truth about me to be the image in my mind. I want the lies that mislead me to become meaningless static. I praise You that You do not leave me to drown in this sea of noise and misinformation, but that Your truth is living and available at any hour of the day or night. I pray that Your Spirit living in me will remind me of Your love, always. Amen.

> *For You formed my inward parts; You covered me in my mother's womb. I will praise You, for I am fearfully and wonderfully made; marvelous are Your works, and that my soul knows very well.*
> PSALM 139:13–14 NKJV

WHAT IS LOVE?

*D*ear Savior and King, we know so little of love. We see love through the dim glass of this world, and it appears pink and cuddly or glowing with passion. Love becomes a preference for one thing over another or a passing whim. We think love is about how we *feel*.

We need You to teach us what love is. Show us what You meant when You said You loved the world so much that You sent Your Son to die for us. Show us what You meant when You said Your love is unfailing and great and endures forever. Show us what You meant when You said love is the fulfillment of the law. Our loves wax and wane, rise and fade; we know nothing of a love that began before the foundations of the world were laid and continues throughout eternity. Forgive us for being content with a shallow understanding of love and a passing commitment to pursuing it. Forgive us for taking it so lightly. We praise You for being a God who abounds and overflows with love. We praise You for loving us while we were Your enemies. Give us soft hearts to love—and be loved—in a way that glorifies You. Amen.

"But you are a God of forgiveness, gracious and merciful, slow to become angry, and rich in unfailing love."
NEHEMIAH 9:17 NLT

The Suffering Servant

*L*ord, You showed Your love with an extravagance of suffering. The prophet Isaiah foretold that You would be crushed, despised, wounded, rejected, punished, stricken, pierced, smitten, afflicted, oppressed, cut off. When the Romans finished with You on Golgotha, You were unrecognizable. And the most crushing blow of all was the incredible weight of all our sins, laid upon You on that cross.

You call us to take up our own crosses daily and follow You, but we don't want to suffer, even in small, insignificant ways. We don't want to fast from a single meal, endure a sleepless night with a sick child, choke back an indignant rebuttal when we are accused, or listen patiently when we'd rather talk. We want to choose our suffering; we want it to be noticed and applauded, and not to hurt too much. But love doesn't get to say, "I will do this for you but not this." Thank You, Lord, that You were willing to do anything to save us. Help us to be servants—faithful, inconspicuous, willing, and humble—no matter how You call us to suffer. We deserve nothing, but You invite us to share in Your suffering and so become like You and live with You forever. What amazing love. Amen.

I want to know Christ—yes, to know the power of his resurrection and participation in his sufferings, becoming like him in his death, and so, somehow, attaining to the resurrection from the dead.
Philippians 3:10–11 niv

About Enemies

_L_ord, when I was younger, I didn't know how full of enemies the world is. I lived in a safe bubble of family and friends and activities, and the rest of the world was far away. Now the world materializes at arm's length; with a click or a tap we learn about troubles, trials, and terror in an instant. We see the faces of those who call themselves our enemies; we see the hatred, fear, and desperation in their eyes. Our enemies are closer now and more numerous. They encroach on us in ways they never did before. And You ask us to love them! Lord, this is a hard teaching, as hard as nails.

But You know all about nails—what they can and can't hold. You chose the nails You used to save the entire world, and You transformed them from a symbol of degradation to a symbol of triumph. I praise You for Your ability to transform _anything_, even me. Through Your Spirit and power living in me, I can do what You ask: I can love my enemies, do good to those who hate me, bless those who curse me, and pray for those who mistreat me. Lord, I believe this. (Help my unbelief.) Amen.

> _"But I say to you who hear, love your enemies, do good to those who hate you, bless those who curse you, pray for those who mistreat you."_
> LUKE 6:27–28 NASB

Speak Life, Speak Life

*D*ear Savior and Friend, voices are everywhere in the world, all the time; silence is rare. We're encouraged to speak up, speak out, speak our mind, say our piece, tell all, express ourselves, let 'em have it. We decide to mow down our opponents with our wit and eloquence, to leave them with their jaws hanging down while the watching world applauds. People who refrain from passing judgment or say, "I don't know," people who don't have a comeback at the ready, are looked down on.

But You say differently, Lord. You were silent before Your accusers, and when You did speak, Your words called weary people to repentance and rest. Your sinless perfection included Your tongue! Help me choke back words that would wound. Help me not say or write the pithy comments I so desire to utter. Help me not talk just to hear my own voice. Help me, instead, speak words of life and love. Help me know when to speak and when to be silent. I know sometimes the most necessary words are no words at all. Let me be a listening ear, a hand that holds and comforts, a shoulder that offers support. I ask, Lord, that if I must speak, You will speak through me. Amen.

Understand [this], my beloved brethren. Let every man be quick to hear [a ready listener], slow to speak, slow to take offense and to get angry.
James 1:19 ampc

An Eternal Sufficiency

*D*ear Lord, before the beginning of the world, You were there. In the perfect equilateral triangle of the Trinity, Father, Spirit, and Son had perfect peace, balance, and communion. Love—the strongest element in the universe—was Your binding force, and You were eternally sufficient, needing nothing besides Yourself.

You say in these verses that nothing can separate me from this love. But I'm scared, Lord—of death, demons, the future, and so many other things. I admit that sometimes I'm even afraid of life, of meeting an angel, of living fully in the present moment, of Your heights and how they might change me. I'm scared of trusting in this promise. I'm scared to go through these things so I can find out Your promises are true. Forgive me for this fear, this lack of trust, this sinful desire to remain small, safe, and separate. Pull me into your eternal sufficiency. You are all-sufficient, and in Christ I partake of that sufficiency. Help me to rest in that, Lord, when fear overwhelms me. Nothing can separate me from Your love. Nothing. Amen.

For I am convinced that neither death nor life, neither angels nor demons, neither the present nor the future. . . nor anything else in all creation, will be able to separate us from the love of God that is in Christ Jesus our Lord.
Romans 8:38–39 niv

AGAINST INDIFFERENCE, PART 1

I'm thinking of love, Lord, and its opposites. Yesterday, two military helicopters flew over my quiet house, so low that the windows rattled, and we ducked for cover. For a second, I panicked. What was happening? Were we at war? The helicopters passed over the trees and into the distance, and in the silence that followed, You convicted me, both of fear and indifference. You reminded me of the incredible, unearned blessing of living in a land of peace and plenty. Thank You for that, Lord. You also reminded me of the millions of people living in war-torn countries, for whom a low-flying helicopter is a daily occurrence. I am so indifferent to those who inhabit continually the fear and uncertainty I felt for just a split second.

Forgive me. Open my eyes to the hurting; incline my ears and heart to their cries. What can I do for them, Lord? What would You have me do? Help me act with the love I would want to be shown in similar circumstances; I know peace and prosperity are fleeting. Thank You for where I am right now, for what might come, and how You promise to be with me always. Amen.

You, Lord, hear the desire of the afflicted;
you encourage them, and you listen to their cry,
defending the fatherless and the oppressed, so that
mere earthly mortals will never again strike terror.
PSALM 10:17–18 NIV

AGAINST INDIFFERENCE, PART 2

$\mathcal{L}$ord, the minute we begin to think about the poor and the oppressed, we realize how full of hurt this broken world is. Pain and sorrow invade every corner of existence. From tiny babies aborted or born malformed; to the elderly, alone and crippled at the end of their days; to young people warped with hate by evil ideologies. Everything and everyone is tainted by the fall, coated with sin. We have so many concerns that it becomes easier to fall into indifference and apathy than to hurt and hurt and hurt again.

Forgive us for being unwilling to hurt with the hurting. We are limited, and You are not. Your love and compassion have no end. In Your omnipotence, You can heal every hurt and wipe away every tear—and You will. We don't know what to do with the sorrows of this world, so we give them to You, Lord. Take them into Your mighty, just, and loving hands. Give us faith that the day You promise—when all those former, terrible things will pass away—is coming, and coming soon. Even so, come, Lord Jesus. Amen.

And God shall wipe away all tears from their eyes;
and there shall be no more death, neither sorrow,
nor crying, neither shall there be any more pain:
for the former things are passed away.
REVELATION 21:4 KJV

HELP MY UNBELIEF

*D*ear Father, if I truly want to know what love is, I need to ask You. You say love believes all things. I ask You to fill me with that kind of believing love. Help me, first, to remember and rehearse what I believe: I believe in God the Father, who created all things. I believe in the Holy Spirit, who lives in me. I believe in the sinless life, death, and resurrection of Your Son, Jesus Christ. I believe You long for our salvation. I believe You are just, and will judge. I believe You are coming again. I believe no one can pluck me out of Your hands. I believe the world was created perfect and will be so again. I believe all the promises You made are fulfilled in Jesus Christ. Jesus is the solution, the key, the remedy. He is the great *Yes*.

Forgive me for not always believing all this, Lord. I want to believe; help my unbelief. And love believes these things are true and necessary in the lives of *everyone,* no matter who they are or where they come from. Show me how this belief can be worked out in my life, and in the lives of those I touch, as love. Amen.

For all the promises of God find their Yes in him.
That is why it is through him that we utter
our Amen to God for his glory.
2 CORINTHIANS 1:20 ESV

You Are the One

*D*ear Lord, You are the One and only, the Alpha and Omega, the beginning and the end, the only name under heaven and earth by which we can be saved. I praise You for Your singularity; You are the only essential thing.

But the world is full of those who say otherwise. Few want to hear that Jesus is the way, the truth, and the life, and that no one comes to the Father except through Him. They insist Jesus is one god among many, one path up the same mountain, one wise teacher among all the other wise teachers who ever lived. My heart aches for their blindness and lostness, Lord. I pray that in Your great mercy, You will open their eyes, ears, and hearts to Your truth before it's too late. I lift to You those who follow false gods, believe in no god at all, or have become their own god. For one day it *will* be too late to choose differently. You will have mercy on whom You will; I pray You will hold back from the brink those who are being saved. Amen.

For we know Him who said, "Vengeance is Mine, I will repay," says the Lord. And again, "The LORD will judge His people." It is a fearful thing to fall into the hands of the living God.
HEBREWS 10:30–31 NKJV

Against Boasting

*D*ear Lord, we know You will have mercy on whom You will have mercy, but as soon as we start thinking of our election, we run the risk of self-righteousness. We begin to think there was some reason—some special skill, talent, or natural disposition—for You to choose us. And then it's just a short mental hop to start elevating ourselves above others. We start thinking we are right and they are wrong.

Whose voice are we listening to when we think that? Is it the voice that whispered in Eden, "Did God really say. . . ?" Or the voice that said in scorn, "Am I my brother's keeper?" Lord, forgive us for this boasting. You tell us love does not boast. We have nothing, and we are nothing. What You gave us is all grace, a gift we didn't deserve. And remind us, Lord, that when we tell of this gift to others, we don't do so in our own strength, but as fellow sinners saved by the same grace—all wanting, all needing, all supplicants at the foot of the cross. If we boast, let us boast only in our weaknesses—and in You. Amen.

For it is by grace you have been saved, through faith—
and this not from yourselves, it is the gift of God—
not by works, so that no one can boast.
Ephesians 2:8–9 niv

BEHOLD WHAT MANNER OF LOVE

*D*ear Father in heaven, You love the unlovable, the orphan, the poor, the friendless—and that's us. You have only one true Son, Jesus Christ, but You are willing to call us all Your children and adopt us into Your family. Only Jesus has Your true nature; the rest of us are aliens and strangers—muddy, filthy, naughty children raised, as it were, by wolves—until You take us in. No natural family of God, no people who belong to You without right or question, no skin color or nationality or language able to claim You as ancestor exists. Black, white, pink, brown, women, children, men—we are all by nature foreigners to You.

But behold Your love! No matter who we are, what we look like when we come to You, where we have been, and what we did there, You are willing to call us *all* Your children. You draw us to Yourself *before* we look anything like Your Son. And that is Your goal as our Father: to have a multitude of children who all resemble Your precious Son. Conform us to *that* image, Father. We praise You, and we pray that You will give us eyes to see one another as those who are being made perfect. Amen.

Behold, what manner of love the Father hath bestowed
upon us, that we should be called the sons of God: therefore
the world knoweth us not, because it knew him not.

1 JOHN 3:1 KJV

Perfect Love Casts Out Fear

*D*ear Father, I am meditating on these verses about your perfect love. Your Word is truth, and Your thoughts are higher than mine. Speak to me, Lord. Show me what these verses mean and how they should change me. You say there is no fear in love. You say perfect love casts out fear. But right now, I admit I'm afraid. These are my fears: I am afraid of growing old before You return. I am afraid of being mocked by those I tell about You. I am afraid those I love will turn away from You. I am afraid those I love will turn away from *me*. I am afraid of pain and loss. I am afraid of a world I cannot control.

Those are the bigger fears. Lesser fears dog me all day long, nipping at my peace. Yet You say "Do not fear" over and over in Your Word. Forgive me, Lord. My love will never be enough to conquer fear; the love You are talking about here is Your own. The more I understand and accept Your love for me, the less room there will be in my heart for fear. Be magnified, Lord, until I rest— unafraid—in Your perfect love. Amen.

There is no fear in love; but perfect love casts out fear, because fear involves torment. But he who fears has not been made perfect in love. We love Him because He first loved us.
1 John 4:18–19 nkjv

LOVE POURED OUT

*D*ear God, Your love is a great mystery; I don't understand why the undergirding nature of the God of the universe is *love*. Why do You love? I don't want to imagine what a universe, built on something other than love, would have looked like. But I'm so thankful that You *are* love and that Your love extends to and encompasses me.

Teach me to rest in that love. I pray that Your love will so fill me and be so real in my life that it will spill out of my eyes, hands, heart, and mouth to everyone around me. Let me bleed love to this hurting world, just like Jesus did. Let me not be afraid of what that might mean: being spilled out for others, and at the same time, having my cup of blessing run over. That seems as though it will feel very different, but maybe it won't! Maybe Jesus' blood spilled out at the cross was also His cup of blessing running over, pouring out on us. This is amazing love; I can hardly comprehend its mystery and majesty. And this is the Spirit's work in me, that I will produce the same fruit. Come, Holy Spirit. Amen.

"Be glad, O children of Zion, and rejoice in the LORD your God, for he has given the early rain for your vindication; he has poured down for you abundant rain, the early and the latter rain, as before."

JOEL 2:23 ESV

SECTION 2: *Joy*

THE LORD IS AT HAND

*D*ear Father, if Your Spirit lives in me, You are always with me. You are the witness to my every thought, word, and action from the moment my mind rumbles into awareness in the morning to my last, half-formed musings at night before sleep overwhelms me. You are with me as I toss and turn in bed; You know my dreams.

Lord, I forget this daily. Forgive me for the grumblings and complaints and vain imaginings that fill my mind when I think I'm alone. Forgive me for the way these negative thoughts shout down and suffocate joy. And forgive me for dwelling in that foul place, instead of immediately fleeing from it. I can't rejoice and complain at the same time. I can't serve those two masters—You and me—at the same time. The last sentence of this passage—*The Lord is at hand*—seems to be the heart of the matter. It tells me You are coming soon, and it also reminds me of my present reality: I am never alone. This both comforts and terrifies me. You hear it all, Lord—both the rejoicing and the bitter complaining. Help me to turn from sin and rejoice. Help me to persevere in practicing that conscious turning away, until my heart learns to sing in harmony with You. Amen.

Rejoice in the Lord always; again I will say,
rejoice. Let your reasonableness be known
to everyone. The Lord is at hand.
PHILIPPIANS 4:4–5 ESV

The Day of Small Things

_L_ord, You ask us to rejoice, but often we don't know what that means. What is joy? Where does it come from? How can we express it in the way You desire? We know it's more than a shallow happiness. It's not pie-in-the-sky-by-and-by. It's not pretending sin and sickness and sadness don't exist. You don't promise us happiness, but You do promise us joy, which is larger and stronger and more miraculous. Joy is the thoroughbass of our life in You, the constant undercurrent of trust and thanksgiving that carries us through rough and dangerous waters. Joy regularly seeks and remembers Your blessings.

Thank You that pain reminds me to pray, Lord. Thank You for drawing me closer to You in that trial. Thank You for using my struggle to help another believer. Thank You for being with me even when I didn't feel You. Thank You for small moments of beauty that remind me of Your presence. Thank You for that song, that verse, that word spoken, all when I needed them. Thank You for a moment of peace in this storm. Help us to do that, Lord—to build a temple of joy, one small stone at a time. Amen.

_"The hands of Zerubbabel have laid the foundation
of this house, and his hands will finish it. Then you
will know that the LORD of hosts has sent me to you.
For who has despised the day of small things?"_
ZECHARIAH 4:9–10 NASB

LIVING WIDE OPEN

*G*racious God, You were the perfect Father to Adam and Eve in the garden of Eden. You gave them everything they could want—purpose, companionship, plenty, beauty. You walked with them in the cool of the day. They had each other, *You*, and a brand-new world, but they still chose to walk out of fellowship with You and into darkness and death. Why, then, do we think our families are going to be any different? Why are we surprised when the people we love reject us and what we believe? Why are we so stunned by how difficult relationships are in this fallen world?

Forgive us, Lord, for so consistently forgetting the severe consequences of sin. You want us to walk with our eyes wide open, despite the dust and dirt and grit that bring us to tears. You want us to walk with our hearts wide open, regardless of what will wound us so deeply that we'll want to die. But to do that we need You. You are our strength and our song. We plead for Your joy, which will allow us to live in that otherwise impossibly vulnerable way. Amen.

Nehemiah said, "Go and enjoy choice food and sweet
drinks, and send some to those who have nothing
prepared. This day is holy to our Lord. Do not grieve,
for the joy of the LORD is your strength."
NEHEMIAH 8:10 NIV

There Is Beauty Still

*D*ear Lord, with our hearts bent on sin, we tend to see everything wrong on this earth: pollution, vanishing species, destruction wrought by severe weather, wildfires, tornados, earthquakes, and floods. But even as the world winds to a close—though we don't know when it will end—we're still surrounded by beauty. Wildflowers spring up from burned places. Crops grow in rich silt brought from a flooded river.

We praise You for the grace that sustains this failing, sinful planet and preserves it while You wait patiently until the time is fulfilled. We thank You for the perfection of a snowflake, for the flash of red at the throat of a hummingbird, for the pink glow of sunset on the flank of a mountain, for a sweet spring breeze, for the early bright heads of daffodils, for the softness of a baby's cheek, for mighty waterfalls cutting through rock. Even though the earth is nothing like it once was—and nothing like it *will* be—there is beauty still. Forgive us for having eyes only for the mars and scars on some days. Help us rejoice, like the angels, in what You have created. It is still good! Amen.

Whereupon are the foundations thereof fastened? or who laid the corner stone thereof; when the morning stars sang together, and all the sons of God shouted for joy?
Job 38:6–7 KJV

JOY FOR MOURNING

$\mathcal{L}$ord, this world seethes with sickness and disease. Every day I hear about someone else who is struggling with illness—anything from a common cold to cancer. So many have died and left behind black holes of grief and loss. Who will be next? When will it end? How much pain and sorrow can we take?

Oh Lord, You hear my cries and the cries of those who suffer. You are the God who heals, Jehovah-Rapha. Your hand of healing is seen all through the Bible. Jesus, You healed people of blindness, paralysis, leprosy, fever, demon-possession, and bleeding throughout Your ministry on earth. You heal people still. I ask for healing, Lord, for all the people I know who are suffering right now: those in my family, my church, my community. But if You don't give them healing in this life, I'll still praise You. Your ways are higher than mine; Your thoughts are deeper than my thoughts. Help me trust that You are in control of even this and that Your purposes *are* prevailing, in this life and the next. When I'm sick or in pain, help me remember how You healed my soul of the sin-sickness that would have killed me, and killed me eternally. To You be all praise and glory forevermore, amen.

> *"To console those who mourn in Zion, to give them*
> *beauty for ashes, the oil of joy for mourning,*
> *the garment of praise for the spirit of heaviness."*
> ISAIAH 61:3 NKJV

Joy, Despite It All

*D*ear Lord, You ask us to be joyful, not just when life is going well—when we're happy, when our relationships are loving and peaceful, when we and our loved ones are healthy, when the bills are paid on time—but also when we're sick, sad, poor, and misunderstood. In these verses, You asked Your people to find their joy in You even when no figs or grapes were on their vines, no olives were on their trees, no crops were in their fields, and no sheep or cattle were in their barns. They weren't finding joy in the barrenness around them; they were finding joy *despite* the barrenness.

Jesus, You found joy in the brokenness and barrenness of this world. As You hung on the cross, You were looking joy right in the eye. It was set before You, and You were going to meet it with Your arms wide open, gathering up all the bitter things as You went—accepting it all, bearing it all, redeeming it all. You are the example set before me of how to live; You are the joy set before me. Thank You, Jesus, that You counted it all joy. Help me to go and do likewise. Amen.

> *Though there are no sheep in the pen and no cattle in the stalls, yet I will rejoice in the L*ORD*, I will be joyful in God my Savior.*
> Habakkuk 3:17–18 niv

Praying to an Empty Sky

Dear God, it seems impossible to pray today. The sky is gray and joyless, and when I think of You, I feel nothing. But I know when I'm tempted to neglect prayer is when I most need to pray. This is when You are molding my soul in obedience, when I do what You ask even though my flesh cries out against it. I want to stop. I am sick of silence and the sound of my own voice. Why are You so far off? Do You hear me?

But this is the faith that counts, my sweet Lord. I will stay here, on my knees, because I *know* certain things about You, even though they don't *seem* true in this moment. You love me. You hear me when I call. You delight in me. You are my Savior. You know what it's like to be human, yet You are perfect. You are eternal, all-knowing, and all-powerful. You draw near to those who seek You. I can love You because You first loved me. Thank You, Lord. The sky is still high and far off, but I know the clouds will blow away to reveal the blue that was always behind them. I know You are there too. Amen.

Hear my voice when I call, LORD; be merciful to me and answer me. My heart says of you, "Seek his face!" Your face, LORD, I will seek.
PSALM 27:7–8 NIV

DON'T STEAL OTHERS' JOY

*D*ear Father, I see people everywhere who speak whatever they want, whenever they want. I hear a world full of noise. People are falling into the pits their own words have created, with others tumbling in after them. I should be different, but I'm not. It's so hard to control my tongue. I pray for patience and wisdom, and I study Your Word, but when I get up off my knees or close my Bible, it's as if I had learned nothing, as if You had never changed me. The words I spew to the first person I see are so often harsh, critical, cynical.

Lord, forgive me. Forgive me. But I feel hopeless sometimes. Am I really being sanctified? Why doesn't it show more? Give me the faith to believe what You have promised is happening. Give me faith to believe You are working in me. Give me faith to believe my sins—even the ones I have just this moment committed—are forgiven. I see the way my unconsidered words rob others of joy. Like You, I want to bring life and light to the people around me. Help me, if not to speak, then to be silent. Amen.

*All things were made by him; and without him
was not any thing made that was made. In him
was life; and the life was the light of men.*
JOHN 1:3–4 KJV

A Joy Beyond Circumstance

*D*ear Lord, You gave Your servant Paul a message for the church in Philippi, and through Your grace and the miraculous preservation of Your Word, we get to read it still. This message was sent to the Philippians then and is sent to *us* now. We marvel, perhaps, that Paul, who wrote it under house arrest in Rome, could have so much to say about joy. But that word, *joy*, rings like a bell throughout his letter. Joy, joy, joy! Rejoice!

Lord, we long for our circumstances to change. We long for the end of fear, anxiety, worry, grief, and suffering. But You long for *us.* Help me to long for You with the same fierce love. Paul endured shipwreck, snakebite, earthquakes, imprisonment, hunger, and poverty, but his eyes were not on himself; he was looking beyond this world to Jesus. Just like Paul says, it is all good, whether we die and depart to be *with* Christ or we remain in the body and perform fruitful labor *for* Christ. Lord, work in our hearts so we truly believe, as Paul did, that our joy is not rooted in our circumstances, but in the unchanging truth and beauty of the Gospel of Jesus Christ. To our God and Father be glory for ever and ever, amen.

[I am] holding fast the word of life,
so that I may rejoice in the day of Christ that
I have not run in vain or labored in vain.
PHILIPPIANS 2:16 NKJV

THE HOLE FILLER

*L*ord, we are surrounded by the most incredible uncertainties. The world teeters with instability; even the words we use can change their meanings daily, it seems, and the meaning we intend to convey may not be what others hear. Language hovers on the edge of incomprehensibility. Still, You know our hearts, and this is a comfort when we're misunderstood. Help us to rest in that.

But beyond that, Lord, we ask You to go before us and our words, to work in the hearts of our hearers, so that, above all, truth is conveyed. Open our ears to what others are saying also. A message always lies beyond their words, which often holds a deeper meaning, a deeper pain, a deeper questioning. Everyone is searching, whether or not they know it. There is, as Pascal said, a God-shaped hole in all of us. Help us to be hole fillers in the truest, deepest sense, pointing others to the God of all joy who will meet their deepest needs. You are the way, the truth, and the life. You are the beginning and the end. You are the Alpha and the Omega. You *were* in the beginning. Really, that truth is all we have to offer others, and it's more than enough. Amen.

Simon Peter answered him, "Lord, to whom shall we go?
You have the words of eternal life. We have come to
believe and to know that you are the Holy One of God."
JOHN 6:68–69 NIV

God Is Enough

*D*ear Eternal Father Strong to Save, nothing seems certain; the ground beneath our feet is unstable, sometimes literally. When we turn on the TV, we never know what devastation, what destruction, we'll hear about. Beautiful places are swept with earthquakes and tsunamis and wars; what's left behind is nothing we recognize. Public figures we always admired are revealed to be fallen, fallible creatures, broken in ways we never imagined. Corruption is uncovered in institutions we trusted. Even in ourselves we find weakness, fear, and anger we never suspected.

Lord, how can we stand in such times? How can we move forward when we don't know if the ground in front of us will hold our weight? We know the answer. We step out in faith, because the only sure thing You promise us in this life is You. Please, Lord, search our hearts and reveal to us whether we believe You are enough. Be magnified in our lives until our idols of peace and comfort and stability are smashed. You are the only rock we can cling to. Amen.

*Let not your heart envy sinners, but continue
in the fear of the LORD all the day. Surely there
is a future, and your hope will not be cut off.*
PROVERBS 23:17–18 ESV

PRISONERS SET FREE

*D*ear Lord, I love this story about Paul and Silas and how the bars of their prison cell did nothing to hold back their joy. With their feet crushed in the stocks, they prayed and sang while all the other prisoners listened and wondered at their joy. They were in chains, yet their souls were freer than anyone around them.

So many people think they're free, Lord, but they're bound by chains of addiction. In the beginning their addictions brought them a sort of counterfeit joy, but over time their pleasure has grown smaller and smaller until nothing is left but joy's shadow and a bitter memory. Lord, I pray for those captives. They can do so little to free themselves. They are trapped by chains they forged with their own hands and then locked onto their bodies themselves. But You are the great chain-breaker. I was fast bound in sin and nature's night when You came into my prison cell, flooded it with heavenly light, and set me free. You can do that again for those in the prison of addiction. Please, shake the ground beneath their feet, crack the walls of their cells, break their chains. And amid the quaking, may Your name be glorified. Amen.

The jailer called for lights, rushed in and fell trembling before Paul and Silas. He then brought them out and asked, "Sirs, what must I do to be saved?"

ACTS 16:29–30 NIV

WHICH PATH?

*L*ord, right now I feel like I'm standing at a fork in the road. Before me are two paths, both leading into the trees. One is wide, smooth, and sunny. The other is shadowed with overhanging branches and rough with roots and rocks. It looks as though no one has gone that way for many years. I don't want to take that path; the other one looks so much more inviting. Surely, they lead to the same place, or nearly so.

But I hear Your voice directing me to that stony path, without any assurance that the rest of the trail isn't as bad as the beginning. "It may be as bad," You say. Lord, give me courage to go down this hard, dark path. Give me faith that it leads to the destination You desire—to You. I'm scared it will be too difficult. I'm scared of being alone where nobody else seems to be traveling. Give me peace and joy as I walk, as I choose You over ease and comfort. Guide my feet and show me in tangible ways that You are walking beside me with every step. Amen.

And your ears will hear a word behind you, saying,
This is the way; walk in it, when you turn to the
right hand and when you turn to the left.
Isaiah 30:21 ampc

FIXING MY EYES

$\mathcal{D}$ear Lord, I praise You when I remember who You are—a God who creates beauty and life, a God who doesn't delight in our sacrifices *yet* was delighted to sacrifice His Son to save us. You are the source of all love, all that is good and true. You desire the salvation of everyone. You hold my present and future and have redeemed my past. You are with me eternally.

Yet even though I know who You are, I confess that my heart wanders from the singular focus You desire. I turn away from You and back to my problems with the mindless regularity of a compass needle. Forgive me for looking away. Forgive me for forgetting that I can see my fears, failures, and struggles rightly only when I'm looking beyond them to You. Thank You for being my true north, for remaining solid and unchanging, in the same position, no matter how far I wander or how dizzy I get from spinning in futile circles of worry. Thank You for the blessings You have given me, which I lose sight of when I'm not looking to You. Thank You for the joy You give, despite circumstances, when my eyes are fixed heavenward. Amen.

> *[Let us fix] our eyes on Jesus, the pioneer and*
> *perfecter of faith. For the joy set before him he*
> *endured the cross, scorning its shame, and sat*
> *down at the right hand of the throne of God.*
> HEBREWS 12:2 NIV

Joy, Joy, Joy

*D*ear God, with the trappings of the Christmas season—twinkling lights, wreaths and decorated trees, glittering wrapping, busyness and buying—it's easy to forget what truly happened all those years ago. Your great heavenly servants, angels so powerful that just one could defeat an entire army, came to earth, and people who saw them fell to the ground in fear. They brought a message no one had ever heard before: God Himself was descending to earth and planning to save all mankind. We were being rescued!

That is truly good news, but *good* hardly seems sufficient, because it's amazing, miraculous, astounding, extravagant, unexpected, staggering news. Ultimately, it's the only news truly good enough to print, the one unchanging fact that will remain long after fads, fetishes, fame, and fortunes all fade into unimportance. Help us keep this Gospel fact at the center of all our celebrations, all year long. Let our banner headline shout: How GREAT OUR JOY! PRAISE TO THE LORD IN HEAVEN ON HIGH. We want so many things, not all of which, if we're being honest, we know will please You. If we have a wish list, Lord, let it be a list of people whose souls need to be saved from the coming destruction. You are the one needful thing. Amen.

But the angel said to them, "Do not be afraid;
for behold, I bring you good news of great
joy which will be for all the people."
LUKE 2:10 NASB

SINGING IN THE SHADOW

*D*ear Father, I praise You for the perfect unity and harmony in the Trinity. You sing a perfect major triad, which has and will reverberate throughout the universe for all eternity. I praise You that heaven rings with music, that the angels sang at the dawn of creation, and that Your throne is surrounded by a great choir of the redeemed. You tell me in Your Word to sing psalms, hymns, and spiritual songs, and I thank You for the reminder of how praise can shape the pattern of my thoughts.

I don't want to be conformed to the pattern of this world, Lord. I don't want my mind molded by trivia, worry, greed, envy, anxiety, fear, or even just by a continual preoccupation with things that will not last. But I am often consumed by these negativities, and I need Your help desperately to know how to turn my fears and failures into songs of praise. Thank You for the example of Your servant David and the hundreds of songs he wrote to You, turning his own fears and failures into praise. With Your help, I can turn sorrow to song and lift my eyes from the earth to the heavens. Praise be to God! Amen.

When I remember You on my bed, I meditate on You in the night watches. Because You have been my help, therefore in the shadow of Your wings I will rejoice.
PSALM 63:6–7 NKJV

Work While It Is Day

*L*ord, the day rushes at me like a panicked child the minute I open my eyes, arms outstretched, crying for help *right now.* If the earth took thirty hours in its turning instead of twenty-four, I still wouldn't have enough time. But I know Your character, and if I want to be like You and retain the joy You give, I need to act as You do. You did not heal every sickness; You did not cast out every demon. You slept. You prayed. You ate. You escaped the insatiable crowds.

Help me discern what You want me to do *right now* among the myriad voices screaming at me, for right now is all I have. It's all I ever have. And my actions in this present moment are either sanctifying me or drawing me away from You. Will I pray—or worry? Will I speak peace—or condemn? Will I help—or hoard my time and energy? This present moment, for good or ill, is Your gift. When obligations press and anxiety whines for my attention, remind me what You said about Your dear friend Mary, who chose to leave the work and worry and sit at Your feet, listening. You said she chose the better part, the one necessary thing—You. Amen.

I must work the works of him that sent me, while it is day: the night cometh, when no man can work.
JOHN 9:4 KJV

The Current of Joy

*D*ear God, You tell me to rejoice, but often I don't know how to start. From where does this rejoicing Paul talks about so freely spring? I know the ability to rejoice in tough circumstances is a gift of Your Spirit. I know—and I thank You—that I can't do it in my own strength. But I also know the work of sanctification in my heart and life is a process in which I am intimately involved. *I can forward it or hinder it.*

So what is my part in this rejoicing? What is the first step toward a life of continual praise? I look to Paul, and I see a man who thanked You constantly, who was confident in You, and who saw everything that happened to him as a means to advance the Gospel of Jesus Christ. Give me the trust to hold my hands wide open to You and to say thank You for whatever comes. Forgive me for my discontent, for nothing kills joy faster. I pray You will teach me to overflow with thanksgiving, so that I can swim in the current of joy. All praise to our great Savior, amen.

Therefore, since we are receiving a kingdom that cannot be shaken, let us be thankful, and so worship God acceptably with reverence and awe.
HEBREWS 12:28 NIV

SECTION 3: *Peace*

GOD OF THE FUTURE

*D*ear Father, You are the God of the past, present, *and* future. You hold everything in Your universe-sized hands, and nothing will surprise You. Nothing disturbs Your peace, perfection, and purpose. We praise You for this aspect of Your divine nature, because time and again we worry and waver. Forgive us for being afraid of the future, for attempting to reject it because it might not be what we want or imagine. You are here, *now*, in this larger, emptier, global world that never sleeps or shuts up.

You are tirelessly aware of everything that goes on— on every device, in every chat room, in every news feed. You know about the cyber threats and bullies, the computer viruses, the scammers, and those who want to steal our identities. We crave Your peace; we beg You to show us what pursuing Your peace really looks like, because resting in You doesn't negate the fact that sometimes we need to *act*. Sometimes we need to rock the boat, disturb the complacency of others, speak hard words into unwilling ears, unplug. Lord, this is so hard to navigate. We put ourselves in Your hands. We pray for wisdom. We pray for peace. We just pray. Amen.

Depart from evil and do good; seek, inquire for, and crave peace and pursue (go after) it! The eyes of the Lord are toward the [uncompromisingly] righteous and His ears are open to their cry.
PSALM 34:14–15 AMPC

Under Almighty Wings

*D*ear Lord, when I opened my eyes this morning to a new day with a bright sun shining in a blue sky, I was reminded what a gift rest is to us. Of course, You neither slumber nor sleep; even though You gave us the example of a Sabbath rest, You don't need to rest. But we do. Our bodies, minds, and souls require it. Thank You for the quiet hours when we can be at peace, silent, still.

Yet often I chafe at my body's need to stop: I want to keep working, I want to stay up late, I want to get it all *done*. Forgive me for neglecting this gift of rest, which is both a command and a blessing. Forgive me for forgetting that resting is an act of faith, a statement about my belief in Your ability to provide for me without my tired striving. And I pray today for those to whom rest does not come easily. I lift those who worry. Teach them to trust. I lift those whose bodies hurt. Bless them with an easing of pain. I lift those who have been dislocated from their homes by war or poverty. Give them shelter. Yet we are truly at peace only under Your almighty wings. Amen.

In peace I will both lie down and sleep, for You, Lord, alone make me dwell in safety and confident trust.
Psalm 4:8 ampc

THE GOD WHO ANSWERS

*L*ord, I'm crying out to You for peace. Today anxiety and worry are gnawing at my soul like rats. I feel like I'm bleeding somewhere deep inside, out of sight. Lord, calm my heart! Give me Your peace, I beg You. Over and over, my mind spins in circles, imagining terrible outcomes and dreadful consequences. Why do I always think the worst thing is bound to happen?

Still this endless, dizzy recitation of my fears. Forgive me for the weak control my faith holds over my mind. You have been my shield and my salvation in times of need for years now. You have always protected, always comforted, always provided. Why do I think You will be any different today? I need You right now, Lord. Like Elijah, I'm crying out to You in a loud voice, arms raised to heaven, with the world watching. Answer me, I pray. Give me Your peace that passes understanding, even if You don't change my circumstances. I will rest here for as long as You desire. And I will proclaim, "The God who answers with peace, He is God!" Amen.

The LORD will give strength unto his people;
the LORD will bless his people with peace.
PSALM 29:11 KJV

Our Peace in a Strange Land

*D*ear God, we are comforted and humbled by how You love us even though we're imperfect. Thousands of years ago, You rescued Israel from slavery with miracle after miracle, yet they still longed to return to the counterfeit peace of Egypt when life got hard. We're no different. Without You, we are slaves who turn to petty comforts to get through each day, trying to ignore the deeper issue of the chains of sin that bind our souls. And even when we've been rescued from those chains by putting our hope in Jesus alone, in some sense we still long to be bound by what is familiar.

Where do we run when trouble comes? Where do our eyes turn first? Enlighten us, Lord, to the mysteries of our own hearts. Show us where our Egypts lie and what are the comforts—the cucumbers and melons of our modern-day existence—to which we are tempted to retreat when the way ahead of us is rough. What do we cry for on difficult days? Is it You, Lord? Let it be. Be our peace in a strange land, which grows stranger by the day. Remind us that You are still our deliverer. Amen.

"I will remember for them the covenant with their ancestors, whom I brought out of the land of Egypt in the sight of the nations, that I might be their God. I am the LORD."

LEVITICUS 26:45 NASB

Widows and Orphans

Heavenly Father, today I heard about a thousand fishermen missing in India after a cyclone ravaged a part of the ocean where such a storm has never hit before. This is tragic on so many levels. Did those men know You, or were they lost to pagan gods? Are any of them marooned or drifting on wreckage? How will the widows and orphans left behind survive without their fathers, husbands, and brothers?

I take comfort in the knowledge that You know the answers to all those questions. I take comfort in the fact that You are both perfectly just and perfectly merciful. We have no hope otherwise. But it's not just in India, Lord, where disasters—as well as war, poverty, accidents, disease, and crime—create widows and orphans. They're created every day in every corner of the globe. I take comfort because I know they are close to Your heart. In so many places, Your Word speaks of Your care for the bereaved and the fatherless. Move my feet, Lord, to minister to the widows and orphans within my reach. Help me to hold my time and treasure lightly so they can be instruments in Your hands. Amen.

*Sing to God, sing in praise of his name, extol him
who rides on the clouds; rejoice before him—his name
is the LORD. A father to the fatherless, a defender
of widows, is God in his holy dwelling.*
PSALM 68:4–5 NIV

The Illusion of Control

*D*ear Lord, the illusion that we're in control of our lives is so persistent. We think we can make everything worrying us turn out the way we want with planning or preparation. We think it is up to us. But there is no peace in that mind-set, because You are not in it. When we reckon without You, it's like trying to exert control in a vacuum: we cannot breathe, we cannot move, and objects float frustratingly beyond our grasp. It's frightening to exist there without You, at the mercy of, really, everything.

But even though we persistently act as though we believe otherwise, we are safe only in Your almighty hands. You are sovereign over every aspect and moment of our lives. Nothing happens outside of Your awareness and authority. As You reassure us through the life of Job, Satan cannot act without Your knowledge and permission, and everything that happens to us—even if it appears evil in the moment—is ultimately for our good. Strengthen our belief in that truth and help us to rest in the peace that comes with right belief. You are air. You are movement. You are life and light. Amen.

"God did this so that they would seek him and perhaps reach out for him and find him, though he is not far from any one of us. 'For in him we live and move and have our being.'"

Acts 17:27–28 niv

What Cannot Be Undone Will Be Redeemed

*P*recious Lord, my sight is so limited. I can't know everything, and I can't see the future that will result from my actions. Yet every day I face choices that will influence my future and the future of others. So often I make those choices in ignorance. I am weak and limited, overwhelmed by the improbability of—until You return—surviving without causing disaster or being the victim of one. I am bowed by this weight, crushed by my smallness. Other times, just like Eve, I want to usurp Your omnipotence, and sin is compounded by sin. When I fail, I long to cry, "I didn't know! It's not fair!"

Forgive me. How can I carry all this responsibility? How can I have peace when I'm buffeted by sin and its consequences? How can I rest in my smallness? Only by recognizing Your greatness. You alone are holy. You alone are all-knowing. You alone are all-powerful. You alone are worthy of praise. Lord, be magnified. Fill my sight so I see nothing else. You can carry it all. You can redeem it all. Take my mistakes—those made in ignorance and those made in willful disobedience—and redeem them. I cast them on You in desperation. No hope or peace is found anywhere but in You. Amen.

"Come to me, all you who are weary and
burdened, and I will give you rest. . . .
For my yoke is easy and my burden is light."
Matthew 11:28, 30 niv

LIFTING TINY ARMS

*D*ear Father, I long to be like a small child, trusting in Your love so much that I stand before You with my arms lifted, knowing You will carry me. Knowing I only need to ask. Knowing You are always there and that You will never leave me. Knowing there will never be a time when, instead of reaching out to me in love, You will push me away with a harsh word.

But, Father, I don't understand divinity. I too often think You are how I see other people: fickle, unpredictable, acting out of selfish motives. Forgive me for not remembering—and believing—what You say about Yourself. You are the One true God; the way, the truth, and the life; my Redeemer; the Creator of the universe; full of mercy; compassionate and long-suffering; the Good Shepherd; my Savior. Forgive me for not remembering what You say about me: that You knew me in my mother's womb, that I was saved out of the flames by Your mighty hand, that I am precious in Your sight. And, Father, I know little ones will form their first opinions about You from my actions. Lend me Your loving, strong arms; let me in faithfulness lift those little ones to You. Amen.

Then he asked them, "But who do you say I am?" Simon Peter answered, "You are the Messiah, the Son of the living God."
MATTHEW 16:15–16 NLT

Trinitarian Peace

*F*ather, Son, Holy Spirit—You need nothing. You are all-sufficient, self-sufficient, self-sustaining, perfect in Yourself, replete. We are so unlike You. We can't imagine the peace of needing nothing, the contentment of that trinitarian existence. We're consumed with needs, wants, and desires from the day we emerge from the womb and our first insistent cries hit the cold air. And all our lives, we are buffeted by our desires, both the legitimate desires of our bodies, minds, and souls and the counterfeit desires of sin. There seems to be no end to our needs and wants, no place of peace between the fulfillment of one desire and the stirring of another.

But You promise in Your Word that You have given us—not *will* give us but *have already* given us—everything we need for life and godliness, everything we need to live and please You. Forgive us for our discontent. We ask that Your promises will be made true in our lives. Help us to live in You, floating equidistant between the Three-in-One, like a baby in its embryonic sac. For where else are we, *really*? Only at the foot of the cross, under sheltering wings, watched over by the Almighty. Keep us here, we pray, in Your infinite mercy. Amen.

His divine power has granted to us all things that pertain to life and godliness, through the knowledge of him who called us to his own glory and excellence.
2 Peter 1:3 esv

Peace on Earth

*D*ear Lord, so often I pray for peace within myself and forget to look beyond my own anxious heart, beyond the struggles in my own relationships. Forgive me for this myopic vision. Today I ask You to spread Your peace over this weary, war-torn world. I pray that Your Spirit will work in the regions of this country and world where strife is bubbling beneath the surface. I pray that Your peace will defuse aggression and usher in reconciliation at every level—from postal clerks to presidents. I pray You will raise up leaders who can think beyond *mine* and *yours* to see our common humanity.

I also pray for the areas where war is raging right now. I pray for Your divine intervention to protect innocent bystanders, preserve homes, and protect precious resources. I pray for misfired guns, misinformation, and misdirection. You confused our languages at the tower of Babel, and You can thwart the plans of the enemy of our souls now. I pray Your Spirit will move mightily in those regions of instability, both to bring about peace and to reveal to the lost that You alone are the Prince of Peace, our only hope amid the conflict of this world. Amen.

"I have told you all this so that you may have peace in me.
Here on earth you will have many trials and sorrows.
But take heart, because I have overcome the world."
John 16:33 NLT

CALLED INTO PEACE

*D*ear Lord, nothing disturbs the divine unity of the Father, Son, and Spirit, and You call Your bride, the church, to partake of that unity. You long for us to be united in belief, purpose, and passion. You long for peace to reign in the pews. But too often that's not what is happening in our churches. Tangential issues grow until they obscure our sight and *You* are lost. Things with no eternal significance become issues upon which churches break and split apart.

That is sin, and we repent of our small minds and hard hearts. We pray for a peace that is larger than—and that can encompass—differences in worship style, baptismal practices, Bible translation, and church structure. Help us to discern rightly when You have a clear opinion about such things and to hold lightly to our personal practices and preferences when Your will on a subject is less clear. Give us hearts that can hold two ideas in tension and still be at peace. Give us grace and love for people who believe differently than we do. Give us the humility to realize we may be wrong. Lord, we open our hands clenched into fists and lift them to You, empty, willing to be filled. Amen.

Behold, how good and pleasant it is when brothers dwell in unity! . . . It is like the dew of Hermon, which falls on the mountains of Zion! For there the LORD has commanded the blessing, life forevermore.
PSALM 133:1, 3 ESV

Doorstep of Heaven

$\mathcal{D}$ear God, You said we would have trouble in this world, and we do. We have no safe place. Shooters invade rural schools and quiet Bible studies, terrorists plow trucks along bike paths and promenades, bombs wait quietly next to the hearts of both the fanatic and the innocent. At any moment, our lives could be over, and we could be seeing You face-to-face, in glory we could never imagine. All our pain and tears and worry and want would be gone, *forever,* as if it had never existed. We would be home, safe.

But not only do You promise to take us to heaven if Your Spirit lives in us when we die, but that You are holding us *now.* We praise You, Lord, for that eternal security. Help us to see the truth that we are in Your hands today, a real, tangible truth, not a promise yet to be fulfilled. In You—right now—we live and move and have our being. Help us see that waiting here, on the doorstep of heaven, is not a precarious place. It's the only safe place, and someday, sooner or later, we will simply step through that door, from life into life. We praise You, Lord of life! Amen.

"Be dressed ready for service and keep your lamps burning,
like servants waiting for their master to return from a
wedding banquet, so that when he comes and knocks
they can immediately open the door for him."
Luke 12:35–36 niv

Concerning Sheep

*D*ear Father, Your Word is truth, and it illuminates both Your character and my own. Without the light it provides, I see myself wrongly: shallow imperfections become grievous faults, and sins masquerade as endearing personal quirks. You become distant, unconcerned, implausible, and powerless. Without the clarity of Your Word, my eyes grow dim, unfocused, and even more nearsighted. Thank You, Lord, for Psalm 23 and what it shows me about who I am, who You are, and how I should relate to You.

But I don't want to be a *sheep*, Lord. That word butts up against my pride and my desire to be self-sufficient and self-determining. Yet I know I *am* a sheep. I am weak, fearful, forgetful, dependent, easily led astray, and longing for a shepherd. Thank You that You are that good shepherd. In this psalm, David sings to me of Your abundance: green pastures, still waters, restoration, plenty, comfort, guidance, protection, goodness, mercy, eternity. And even when my eyes are hazy with fear and confusion, You walk beside me in that darkness. Teach me, Lord. Speak to me. Lead me. Help me immerse myself in Your Word until it becomes the filter, the lens, the medium through which I see. Help me to hear and obey Your precious voice. I yearn for it above all others. Amen.

The Lord is my shepherd; I shall not want.
He makes me to lie down in green pastures;
He leads me beside the still waters.
Psalm 23:1–2 nkjv

PEACE FOR THIS MOMENT

*D*ear Lord, I praise You today for where You have placed me. I would not have chosen what You have given me in this moment, but You made this choice for Your divine purposes. I praise You for Your wisdom, gentle guidance, and the strong hand with which You lead me. I praise You for Your promise to mold me into the image of Your Son. I repent of my complaining heart, which seeks its own way, not Yours. I repent of wanting comfort more than sanctification and affirmation more than truth. I repent of my anger and impatience with the people and circumstances before me, instead of seeing them rightly, as engineered by You for Your own good purposes.

I thank You for what You have given me today. Help me to be an instrument of grace in the lives of others; let me be Your hands, gentle and loving and sure. Let me speak and act with a peace that passes understanding. This peace, Lord, is supernatural; nothing in me can attain it or even imagine what it looks like. Only Christ, living in me, brings this peace. I renounce my agenda for today, and I open my heart, yielded and still, to You. Amen.

I have learned the secret of living in every situation,
whether it is with a full stomach or empty,
with plenty or little. For I can do everything
through Christ, who gives me strength.
PHILIPPIANS 4:12–13 NLT

ON THE RAZOR'S EDGE

*L*ord, some say Your will is a razor's edge, with a sharp precipice on either side and no room for missteps. Others say it's a particular set of circumstances and behaviors—the God spot, which I might miss if I'm not paying close attention, and then I'd be out of Your will. Who knows what blessings I might miss and what terrible things might happen as a result?

But the longer I know You, Father, the less I'm trapped by that capricious view of Your nature. Your will is as wide as Your mercy, and I find great peace there. Yes, Your Word does show You gave particular messages to certain people, asking them to take specific actions. You could, as You told Jonah to go to Nineveh, tell me to go someplace like Minneapolis and preach. If You do, Lord, help me go, immediately. But Your Word also speaks to me in much broader ways—less where to go and what to do, and more who You are and how that should change me. Knowing Your will flows directly from the fountain of knowing You. Please reveal Yourself to me in Your Word, and conform me into the image of the invisible God so I *will* do Your will. Amen.

> *"This, then, is how you should pray: 'Our Father in heaven, hallowed be your name, your kingdom come, your will be done, on earth as it is in heaven.'"*
> MATTHEW 6:9–10 NIV

GLORY ONLY IN YOU

*D*earest Lord, I praise You today for how Your creation shouts of Your power, glory, and beauty. Such delight and awe could never be produced by random chance and time. Beauty—and our ability to recognize it—can come only from You. Thank You for giving us the capacity to delight and for how deep that gift runs in our souls. Thank You that if I lost my sight, I could still hear birdsong and gurgling brooks and wind through poplar leaves. If I lost my hearing, I could still feel the intricacies of a flower with my fingertips and smell its perfume. Even without sight, hearing, touch, and smell, I could still contemplate You and Your beauty in my mind. And if my brain was ravaged by disease or age, I would still be valuable simply because You created me.

Do ants thank You for the ability to work, or glory in the busy humming of their nests and the magnificence of their queens? Does a seagull praise You for the wind and the shape of its wings? But, today, I have lips and a tongue and a mind to praise You. You spoke the world into being. Who is like You? Praise be to God! Amen.

For You, O LORD, have made me glad by what You have done, I will sing for joy at the works of Your hands. How great are Your works, O LORD! Your thoughts are very deep.

PSALM 92:4–5 NASB

Lifted

*D*ear Father, I ask for peace today, for who I am, bunions and all. I ask for peace with the talents You have given me; may I use them for Your glory. I ask for peace with what I don't do well; may I offer my limitations as a sacrifice of praise. You alone are God, and I see Your power at work in this impatient, unloving, self-focused, and petty creature I am. Every act of love, every peaceful word, every thought that reaches toward You is a miracle of Your power at work in me. I praise You for being so willing to insert Your Spirit into Your creature. You don't hold Yourself aloof. You don't crush me in my sins and rise on my broken bones. Instead You enter and give me Your own strength without counting the cost.

Lord, thank You for giving me peace in my weakness. Thank You for Your strong, loving arms. I know I can walk no further without You. I stand here at the foot of the cross, from which Your broken body hangs, in utter peace, my arms lifted in supplication and praise. Amen.

And he said unto me, My grace is sufficient for thee: for my strength is made perfect in weakness. Most gladly therefore will I rather glory in my infirmities, that the power of Christ may rest upon me.
2 Corinthians 12:9 kjv

GUARDED BY PEACE

*D*ear Lord, we long for our hearts and minds to be guarded by the peace You speak of in Philippians 4:7. Yes, we know that both troubles we cannot anticipate and troubles we'll not be able to overcome will come in this life. But a peace that's the result of safety and comfort is not the peace You show us here. You offer a peace that defies worldly explanations, a peace unbelievers will see and wonder at, a peace we will not understand ourselves. It's *Your* peace, God, and it will be a bastion for our minds and hearts against whatever trouble we face.

You say this peace surpasses all understanding: it is both larger and more inexplicable than we can possibly know. It's like You, Lord. You are not a god conceived by human minds, small enough to hold and turn in our hands and look at from every angle. You hold *us*, and You know us as thoroughly as a potter knows the angles, imperfections, and beauties of every pot he has fashioned. We praise You for Your largeness and mystery. We praise You for the promises You hold out to us in Christ Jesus. We stand amazed and humbled at who You are and how You stand guard over us. Amen.

And the peace of God, which surpasses all understanding,
will guard your hearts and minds through Christ Jesus.
PHILIPPIANS 4:7 NKJV

SECTION 4: *Patience*

GOD IS WAITING

*G*od, the world waited for Your coming two thousand years ago, and it waits again. Those of us who know You are impatient for Your return. We look to the sky with longing; our ears are listening for that last, unmistakable trumpet call. But Your patience and love for the lost are greater than our longing. You are not willing that any should perish, and You are waiting, waiting, until the number is fulfilled, until all have heard.

That long-suffering love is hard to understand. We humans give up on loving; we move past the wayward spouse, the prodigal child, and think it's a sign of growth. You, Lord, hate sin with all Your being, yet You are willing to let it continue because You love us so much. The earth is full of murder, rape, theft, cruelty, adultery, and yet Your love is larger and longer than it all. You will not be hurried; You will not be hindered. Your patience stretches—as does Your love—from sky to sky, from the beginning to the end of days. We praise You for that patience, how it waited for us and now waits for others. Give us, Lord, that long view as we learn to love in these last days. Amen.

"And he will send his angels with a loud trumpet call,
and they will gather his elect from the four winds,
from one end of the heavens to the other."
MATTHEW 24:31 NIV

Wait for Me

$\mathcal{T}$oday I am impatient with the slowness of my sanctification, Lord. I want to be perfect—*now*—but I keep sinning, over and over, in the same frustrating ways. I lose my temper with those close to me. I speak callously to people I don't know. I choose myself over others. I act without thinking of You. I complain and mutter like a spoiled child instead of praying. I keep my salvation to myself as though it isn't the greatest gift in the world.

Lord, I know Your purposes will not be thwarted—and that's true in my small life as well as in the larger purposes and plans You have for this world. Thank You that You are working in me all the time, even when I feel like nothing is happening or that I'm not making positive progress toward You. Help me to press in to You and to constantly turn back when my sin pulls my gaze away from You. I thank You that Your love is so patient. You have suffered long for me. Thank You for not giving up. Help me be patient with myself too. Change is hard, Lord, but I am not who I once was. And I am not who I will be when I finally see You face-to-face. Amen.

> *May God himself, the God of peace, sanctify*
> *you through and through. . . . The one who*
> *calls you is faithful, and he will do it.*
> 1 Thessalonians 5:23–24 niv

If We Follow On

*D*ear Lord, we praise You that You are a God who calls us to know Him. You do not hold Yourself far off, but stand at the door, knocking, ready to enter. You are *Abba*, Father, Friend. Those words are so intimate, and we marvel that the eternal, omnipotent, invisible Creator of the universe is our *daddy*.

Promises are in this verse: You *shall come*, and we *shall know*. They are as certain as the promise that spring rain will come again, though now the earth waits, thirsty. Our souls are thirsty for You too. They are cracked and broken, longing for the clear refreshment of Your Spirit to soften the rough, dry places; to soothe; to fill; and to begin the greening process in our hearts. Only You can accomplish this. Give us patience as we wait for You, Lord. Help us draw near to You, follow on to know You, and be zealous to cherish You. This is not a quick process You ask us to undergo, but a long dedication to pursuing You. We will pursue You until we see You. Give us Your strength to be this patient, this long-suffering, this faithful. In Jesus' name we pray and live, amen.

Then shall we know, if we follow on to know the Lord: *his going forth is prepared as the morning; and he shall come unto us as the rain, as the latter and former rain unto the earth.*
Hosea 6:3 kjv

Sabbath Rest

*D*ear Lord, we praise You today for the gift of rest. You are not like the gods of this earth who ask their followers to *work* and *do* and *try* without ever saying, "It is finished." They wonder if they will ever please their god enough to merit salvation, but we know we can never do enough to merit salvation. And instead of producing hopelessness, that gives us the greatest peace. You love us simply because we are Your children, and You welcome us into Your rest with open arms.

Yet so often we neglect to rest. We think our effort is what advances Your kingdom, and we think the quality of our concentration is what keeps our lives from careening out of control. Forgive us. Help us to pause and wonder at the beauty around us, to marvel at the creatures and people You have made, to praise You for the way You care for us. In Christ alone is our hope, our peace, our rest. He is Your gift to us and the spinning world. Help us to stop, take this great gift, and taste and see that You are good. This is the difference between *do* and *done*. Amen.

So there remains a Sabbath rest for the people of God.
For the one who has entered His rest has himself also
rested from his works, as God did from His.
Hebrews 4:9–10 nasb

COME THOU FOUNT

*D*ear Father, when we are weary and dry, we turn to You. When we have no words to pray, our souls are craving the obedience of praise, whether or not we realize it. You promise us days of refreshing and revival will come if we call on Your name. So we ask for that today.

We turn our hearts to You, Lord. Hear us. Speak words of comfort and love and truth to our souls. Quiet our buzzing minds so we can hear Your voice in return. We praise You for being almighty, being perfect, working wonders large and small. We pray that through the act of praising You, we will see and love You more clearly. Be magnified. Fill our hearts. Revive our love, and do not let us grow cold. You are the fount of every blessing, and we long for our hearts to be instruments tuned to give You praise. Praise is the natural outpouring of a thankful heart, so remind us of Your blessings, daily. Thank You for our bodies, our minds, our souls, our strength. They were given so we could love You and praise You. Use us, Lord, as living temples of praise to our great God. Amen.

"Repent therefore and be converted, that your sins may be blotted out, so that times of refreshing may come from the presence of the Lord."
ACTS 3:19 NKJV

LIVING IN THE VALLEY

*D*ear Lord, I'm feeling discouraged today with all I have to do and how hard it all is. I want comfort and ease and a smooth path, but You are giving me sickness, sleepless nights, and difficulties that seem to multiply far beyond the time and energy I have to deal with them. I don't know how to live here, where You have placed me, in a way that pleases You.

But I know You have not abandoned me, regardless of how I feel. I cast my cares upon You, Lord, because You say You care for me, and right now I choose to believe You. You are bigger and stronger than anything I face, and as strange as it sounds, You gave these struggles to me for a good purpose. So I'm making a choice to thank You. You are asking me to stay here and walk through this. Mountaintops are amazing, but I can't live there. The valleys are where I grow and learn what it means to follow You. I pray for patience and a glimpse of You walking beside me. I think of Jesus, walking along dusty Galilean roads with His disciples, and I know You are also with me. Emmanuel. Amen.

Even when I walk through the darkest valley,
I will not be afraid, for you are close beside me.
Your rod and your staff protect and comfort me.
PSALM 23:4 NLT

WAIT

*L*ord, we want things done now, or *yesterday*. The speed of life—with cars, airplanes, electronic communication, online shopping, cell phones, instant access to answers to the most obscure questions—has made waiting a thing of the past. And that desire for instant gratification contaminates our faith. We pray and expect an answer *now*. We read Your promises in the Bible and expect them to be fulfilled for us *today*. We forget You don't always work that way.

Forgive us for trying to make You into who we want You to be instead of being willing to learn more of who You are. Thank You for the people in Your Word who show us the time frame in which You often work. Thank You for Joseph, who waited, forgotten, in prison for years. Thank You for Abraham, who waited decades for the child You promised him. Thank You for the Jews, who waited centuries for their redeemer. Thank You for the early Christians who waited their entire lives for Your return. Thank You that we are waiting still. Teach us that patience isn't passivity, but allowing the other to choose; it's giving time for You to work. Prayer is the active, patient place where free will and divinity intersect. And in the waiting, we are changed. Thank You for that work in our lives. Amen.

Bear in mind that our Lord's patience means salvation,
just as our dear brother Paul also wrote you
with the wisdom that God gave him.
2 PETER 3:15 NIV

Justice Is Coming
Like the Sunrise

_D_ear Lord, as Your people have always done, we cry out, "How long?" How long until Your kingdom comes and Your will is done, here, as it already is in heaven? How long will Your people suffer for following You? How long will corrupt leaders mistreat the innocent and pervert justice? How long will You suffer fools to reign and prosper? We are waiting for You to execute judgment and justice on the earth. We know You see it all: the corruption, foolishness, scandal, and violence. You are not blind.

Yet You are patient, and You want us to be patient too. In our waiting, Lord, show us how to live. Show us how to both respect the leaders You have put over us and to work for godly change in high places. Show us how to pray. Show us how to act. We need Your wisdom when so much seems or is wrong, when we seem so powerless. But we know—with wonder and thanksgiving—that in Christ, we are not powerless. Just like the believers at Pentecost, we have power from on high. Teach us to use it with both faith and faithfulness. Keep us from throwing up our hands in despair. Keep us from responding to injustice in this world with anything but Your grace, love, and truth. Amen.

Behold, the days come, saith the LORD, that I will raise unto David a righteous Branch, and a King shall reign and prosper, and shall execute judgment and justice in the earth.
JEREMIAH 23:5 KJV

The Slowness of God

*D*ear Lord, You are never in a hurry. You create and redeem in Your time. You never rush to judgment or act rashly. You never need to retract anything You've said or done. Your only regret is our sin—and even in that, You offer salvation. Even Your perfectly justified, righteous anger at the way we turn our backs on You does not end there. Instead, it turns to love and ends at the cross.

Thank You, Lord, for that great, patient love. We want to love like You do, but our anger kindles in an instant. Hot words flash out and wound. Bitterness smolders under the skin; we seethe and need only a spark or a puff of air to burn. Your holy fire purifies, but the fire of our tongues is uncontrolled, demonic, and destructive. It brings only death. We ask You, instead, for life. We can't control the rash words or actions of others, but with the enabling of Your Spirit, we can control our own. Teach us to wait, to listen, to invite. Teach us to love those who wound us and not forsake them. Pour Your love on our sinful anger, Lord, until we are filled with the ready forgiveness only You can give. Extinguish everything but love. Amen.

> *"But you are a God ready to forgive, gracious*
> *and merciful, slow to anger and abounding in*
> *steadfast love, and did not forsake them."*
> Nehemiah 9:17 esv

Faith Enough to Bear Me Up

*D*ear Father, as I meditate on these verses, I see faith described as a force with weight, strength, and power far beyond my conception. Too often I think simple faith is for old ladies, children, or the sick—people limited in what they can *do*. I think I will prove the fervency of my faith by some bold deed done in Your name.

But while it's true that faith without works is dead, no works are possible without faith. Faith is first. Faith is not some gossamer net, insubstantial and easily torn. It can move mountains. It is enough for the righteous to *live* on. If we can live on faith, that means it provides everything we need. Faith is nourishment, shelter, safety, love, meaning, purpose, calling. That provision is solid ground and a richness of relationship beyond my expectation or experience. You are so much more than what I know. You are infinite, and I have only to ask for what I need. Increase my faith. Reveal Yourself to me, so that when I am old—and already I am hastening to my end on this earth—my faith *will* move mountains. Amen.

For still the vision awaits its appointed time;
it hastens to the end—it will not lie. If it seems slow,
wait for it; it will surely come; it will not delay. . . .
"but the righteous shall live by his faith."
Habakkuk 2:3–4 esv

You Too

*L*ord, I take great comfort in the fact that, although You are God and Creator of this universe, You were also a man. You walked miles along dusty roads until Your feet were dirty and sore. You felt the sorrow of losing a friend before his time. You were hungry and tired and thirsty. You felt fear, regret, and longing. You were tempted to sin. You are Emmanuel—God with us. You were here on this earth and lived just like us, immured in a human body.

I praise You for the Incarnation—God becoming flesh—and what that means for my relationship to my Creator. You are so kind, Lord, to take on the burdens and limitations of flesh. You are so patient to be willing to walk at the disciples' pace along the lakeshore. You are so loving to both require a payment for sin and be willing to pay that debt Yourself. When I'm tired, I remember You needed to rest. When I'm sad, I remember You cried. When I'm tempted, I remember You were tempted too. And when I fall, I remember You have already paid the price for my sin. Amen.

But when the fullness of the time came, God sent forth His Son, born of a woman, born under the Law, so that He might redeem those who were under the Law, that we might receive the adoption as sons.

Galatians 4:4–5 nasb

I Have Never Been Alone

*B*ut, Jesus, knowing that You also felt tired, sad, and fearful doesn't always make me feel *better*. I want You to take away those feelings. I want the pain, trouble, and struggle to stop. I want to be rested and well and happy and content. That's what I want, and right now the fact that You also felt those things doesn't help. I'm asking, "So what? How does that change how I feel? How should it?" And I'm sorry for the bitterness of my prayer. I'm listening for Your voice. Speak, Lord.

Immediately, I'm reminded of the verses that say You are walking with me. Your Word says You put me here for Your good purposes and *mine*, and that You know all about my struggles. It's still hard, Lord, but the hardness has changed slightly. Now my struggle is more like the grueling ache of a long climb to a mountain peak or the sweat and pain of a muscle worn-out so it can become stronger. Thank You for being *right there*, Lord. Before the words had even left my lips, You were answering. I am not alone. I have never been alone. All praise and thanks to my comforter, healer, and friend. Amen.

Because thy lovingkindness is better than life,
my lips shall praise thee. Thus will I bless thee
while I live: I will lift up my hands in thy name.
Psalm 63:3–4 kjv

PATIENCE FOR PEOPLE

*D*ear Father, please give me patience with the people You have given me—my children, relatives, loved ones, and friends. Our sinful edges rub against each other and chafe when they're not cushioned by forgiveness and love. I sigh and fret, impatient for Your work to be done in their hearts, even while I'm fighting against Your work in me. And when I'm being honest, I realize my desire for the salvation of others is made up in large part of selfishness and pride, not a concern for their eternal souls.

Forgive me, Lord. Give me a willingness to be inconvenienced and humbled in the service of others. Give me the ability to wait for You to act. I can do nothing except love and be a witness to the work You have done in my life anyway. Salvation is Your work alone and accomplished in Your time. I praise You in advance for Your perfect timing. I hope for what I don't yet see in their lives, and I will wait for it with patience, knowing Your longing for them is greater than mine and that Your longing will draw them in and produce the repentance that leads to salvation. Amen.

For in this hope we were saved. Now hope that is seen is not hope. For who hopes for what he sees? But if we hope for what we do not see, we wait for it with patience.
ROMANS 8:24–25 ESV

THE MISSING ONES

*D*ear Lord, we pray today for those who are wrenched by grief. Death had no place in Your original plan; the garden of Eden had no shadow of loss until sin slipped in with the serpent. Our broken hearts in death's presence show it is Your enemy and foreign to Your life-giving nature. Everything in us cries out against it.

Please fill the void in those who have lost people dear to them. Be a father to the fatherless and the lover of the souls of those who are widowed and alone. Meet their needs, Lord, and spur us to be Your hands and feet. We also ask You to prepare us for the days of grief that may come in our own lives. If it's Your will, we ask You to protect our loved ones, but we also ask You to increase our faith and dependence on You *now* so that if tempests come and our eyes are blinded with tears, our feet will stand firm on the rock of our salvation. We praise You, Lord, that we will see our departed loved ones again, and we long for the day when we will see You—and those we've lost—on eternity's side of the veil. Amen.

So we don't look at the troubles we can see now;
rather, we fix our gaze on things that cannot be seen.
For the things we see now will soon be gone,
but things we cannot see will last forever.
2 Corinthians 4:18 nlt

Behind and Before

*L*ord, the deception of self-determination is smashed in this verse, and we rejoice knowing that You go before us and guard our backs. You are walking ahead of us into whatever is coming, unsurprised and all-powerful. You guard us in ways we never even realize: invisible hedges surround us, and angels hover near, though we are unaware of their presence. Nothing can breach those sure defenses without Your knowledge and permission, and we praise You for Your infinite care and ceaseless awareness of us. We cannot run ahead of You or lag behind You, out of sight. You encircle us.

Help us to rest in the cup of Your hands, to stop our childish struggling to be put down. And as we learn to rest, we realize people near us have at times called out for help, but we didn't hear them. Or worse, we were too tired or preoccupied to answer. Remind us, even in that, how insufficient we are to be the guards and rescuers of others. Forgive us, Lord. Sharpen our ears and quicken our feet. Only You are always on watch. We pray for Your continued care and protection. We ask for a glimpse of the unseen wings and walls that encompass us, so that our trust and the praise that overflows from it will increase. Amen.

*But you will not leave in haste or go in flight; for the L*ord *will go before you, the God of Israel will be your rear guard.*
ISAIAH 52:12 NIV

For the Burdened

*D*ear Father, I pray for those who are burdened beyond what they think they can bear. I pray for pastors, struggling under the weight of responsibility for many souls. I pray for parents who despair of their children's salvation. I pray for caregivers meeting need after need, with no one to ask what *they* need. I pray for those facing the continual stresses of sickness, financial struggles, and loneliness.

These are heavy weights, Lord. I lift those who bear them up to You because I don't know how else they can continue. Your strength is their only hope and consolation, the only resource that will never be depleted, the only well that will never run dry. I pray they will feel Your presence in lonely nights and long days. I pray You will be, as You promise, the lifter of their heads when they are tired, discouraged, or hopeless. I pray You will give them strength to go on. Send them help and a joy that comes only from You. Teach them patience and perseverance and what it means to walk in Your strength and not their own. Give them moments of peace to pause and calmly think about that! Amen.

But You, O Lord, are a shield for me, my glory, and the lifter of my head. With my voice I cry to the Lord, and He hears and answers me out of His holy hill. Selah [pause, and calmly think of that]!
Psalm 3:3–4 ampc

See How the Farmer Waits

*W*e wait, Lord, for so many things: birthdays, holidays, visits, new babies, milestones, vacations. We have so much to look forward to, and we thank You for the blessings You have given and the ones You will give. You are a generous, loving Father.

But we wait for other things with dread, not eagerness: possible rejection or failure, test results, death. Strengthen us in this waiting to believe in Your love and care even when our lives seem to be falling apart. Unlike gods of silver, wood, and stone, You are never absent; You are never too deep in thought to hear us; You are never asleep. Because You are the true and living God, You are always aware of us and always at hand. If we truly understood that, we would have no sense of waiting. But we are visceral creatures who long to touch and be touched, to see and be seen. You made us this way, so the longing we feel is also from You. Thank You for how that desire draws us to You. Help us find contentment in the tension between *now* and *then*. You are here. You are coming. They are both true, and so we praise You. Amen.

Be patient, then, brothers and sisters, until the Lord's coming. See how the farmer waits for the land to yield its valuable crop, patiently waiting for the autumn and spring rains.
James 5:7 niv

The Real Struggle

*D*ear Lord, when I struggle with relationships—when I bump up against sharp elbows and even sharper tongues—it's good to remember my struggle is not with those flesh-and-blood people. They are Your creatures, just as I am. The true war is against the enemy of my soul, Satan, who rules this dark world for a time because he's allowed to.

Thank You, Lord, for showing me my adversary and detailing how to fight. Give me patience and perseverance as I learn to arm myself with Your weapons. I pray for truth to be buckled around me so I won't step beyond it in anything I say. I pray for righteousness to guard my heart from lies. I pray for well-shod feet, able to stand their ground and eager to step out in service to the Gospel. I pray for a faith shining before me, visible and effective and as real as an iron shield. I pray that my salvation will guard me like a helmet and that the sword in my hand will be Your Word. I don't look like a warrior, Lord; I live an ordinary life. But You see me as I really am—girded, ready, and enabled by Your Spirit. Amen.

For our struggle is not against flesh and blood,
but against the rulers, against the authorities,
against the powers of this dark world and against
the spiritual forces of evil in the heavenly realms.
Ephesians 6:12 niv

SECTION 5: *Kindness*

THE LOVING-KINDNESS OF GOD

*D*ear Lord, in You, virtues are not abstractions. In You, they come to life and take on flesh and personhood. We think of kindness and love as light and airy, perfect to adorn a greeting card. But in You, they became, quite literally, the body and blood of Your Son. When Jesus appeared as a man, He was the embodiment of Your kindness and love.

We think of kindness and love as what we can do for others—making nice gestures, giving friendly smiles, sharing a basket of muffins, spending an hour raking leaves. But Your kindness was so much more than that. It cried, it prayed, it was tortured, it bled, it died, and it rose again. We can do nothing to add to that. Your kindness and love have already done it all. Your kindness and love alone save us. Forgive us for minimizing and trivializing those virtues. Your kindness, Lord, is this: You know us completely and yet are sympathetic toward us, forbearing and gentle. Your love is this: You took our punishment and accept us as Yours based on nothing but that. You require us to bring nothing. We come naked, helpless, hollow. You clothe, empower, and redeem. We praise You for Your kindness and love. Amen.

But when the kindness and the love of God our Savior toward man appeared, not by works of righteousness which we have done, but according to His mercy He saved us.

TITUS 3:4–5 NKJV

SUCH WERE SOME OF YOU

*L*ord, in these days of foolishness and prosperity, I find it easy to hate. I look at the faces shouting on television and over the internet, distorted with self-righteous indignation and anger, and I think, *I am nothing like that.* In my abundance, I forget the starvation of the godless soul. I forget what I once was—lost, broken, despairing. I forget that until You showed me my sinfulness and utter worthlessness beside You, I was just as full of self-righteousness and wind and noise. And I forget that still, without Your Spirit, I judge without knowledge and harbor anger. I see others only in relationship to *me*, not in relationship to *You*—the only way I can see them rightly.

Are they far from You? Are they searching? Are they hurting? What would You say to them if they were listening? Help me hear with Your kind ears and see with Your kind eyes. Jesus, You look on the lost with compassion because they are like sheep without a shepherd—bleating, confused, scared. I praise You for rescuing me, for washing me in Your blood, for sanctifying me, for justifying me. All praise to our saving Lord. Amen.

Such were some of you; but you were washed, but you
were sanctified, but you were justified in the name of
the Lord Jesus Christ and in the Spirit of our God.
1 CORINTHIANS 6:11 NASB

SUSPICION

$\mathcal{D}$ear Lord, I'm afraid of what I don't know, and my ignorance far outweighs my knowledge. I've lived in my little bubble for years and years, through no fault of my own, really—just an accident (are there any accidents?) of geography and nation. The people around me, for the most part, look just like me, and that is comfortable. And thank You, Lord, for letting me live safe in this sheltered place, far from the turmoil and danger in so many parts of this world.

But even as I rest in ease, it has drawbacks. It makes me timid because I'm not forced to rely on You daily. It makes me complacent because I'm not forced to confront difficult issues in anything but the most abstract sense. Help me, Lord, to identify and sympathize with the marginalized and oppressed, because if I truly live like You've called me to live—*in* the world but not *of* the world—I'll be an alien and a stranger here as well. Help me enter the experiences of others so I can know and share with confidence that You are a God for all people, all places, and all times. Amen.

All these people died still believing what God had promised them. They did not receive what was promised, but they saw it all from a distance and welcomed it. They agreed that they were foreigners and nomads here on earth.
HEBREWS 11:13 NLT

HOLDING ME

*D*ear Lord, right now I'm worrying about the future. I know this worry is a sin, but I'm like an addict who hates her poison yet can't walk away from it. Somehow, I think worry prepares me for the future, but it prepares me only for a future apart from You. This is what worry says to You: "I'm rejecting the blessings You're giving me right now; I don't trust You, and I don't think You have my good in mind. I think You are going to leave me and forsake me." When I worry, I'm flirting with being forsaken in my mind, testing what a life without You would be like, believing the lies that my life could be barren, broken, hopeless.

The way it feels when I imagine that godless world should make me run back into Your arms like a lost child, found. And I do want You, close and alive and speaking into my heart as though You are living there. I want Your Word like a spring breeze, clearing the choking dust from my soul. You are so kind, Lord, to take the terrible weight of the future and hold it for me. Help me remember that You are always holding it—and me. Amen.

How excellent is thy lovingkindness, O God!
therefore the children of men put their trust under
the shadow of thy wings. . . . For with thee is the
fountain of life: in thy light shall we see light.
Psalm 36:7, 9 kjv

INTERLUDE OF PRAISE

*D*ear Lord, I want to boast in You alone, to tell of Your beauty and goodness to all who will listen, to remind myself of Your faithfulness. It is good to praise You, for You are good. I praise You for music, mountains, grass, streams, moss, birds, trees, and flowers. *You are loving.* I praise You for babies, kisses, and all things with fur. *You are righteous.* I praise You for both requiring and enabling perfection through the perfect sacrifice of Your Son. *You are eternal.* I praise You that there was never a time when You weren't brooding over the world and loving it. *You are all-knowing.* I praise You that there is nothing outside of Your awareness. You see every anxious thought, every evil deed, every act of love. *You are all-powerful.* I praise You that You have already won the battle and are just waiting for the last captives of the enemy to be returned home before the eternal celebrations begin. I could sing and shout of Your name, Your praise, Your salvation!

It is good to praise You, Lord. Thank You for the joy of reorienting my mind to You. Remind me often to lift my hands in awe and wonder. Amen!

> *I will extol the Lord at all times; his praise will always be on my lips. I will glory in the Lord; let the afflicted hear and rejoice. Glorify the Lord with me; let us exalt his name together.*
> PSALM 34:1–3 NIV

RESPECT AND LOVE

*D*ear Father, we ask Your help today to offer respect and love, not criticism. So often we think we know best about virtually everything: family life, politics, history, domestic policy, international relations, corporate management, Bible interpretation, and everything under the sun. We even think we know all about You. But You are beyond searching out. Much of what we think we understand is beyond searching too. This world and its history are so complicated, and to recognize that and the limits of our experience and knowledge is a just humility.

We ask You to remind us of our smallness and give us the grace to accept it. Please, Lord, stop our endless words, our excuses and justifications and defenses of our own virtue and intelligence. Give us respect for other viewpoints and love for those who hold them. Let us be willing not only to say, "I don't know," but also "I was wrong" and "You're right." Let us be willing to praise others. Let us be willing to ask, to listen, to understand. Open our hearts to learn from those around us; give us rest from self-righteousness. We praise You that You can use other fallible, sinful creatures in forming us to be like the Perfect One, Jesus Christ. Amen.

Trust in the LORD with all your heart; do not depend on your own understanding. Seek his will in all you do, and he will show you which path to take.
PROVERBS 3:5–6 NLT

THE THREEFOLD CORD

*D*ear God, we think there is virtue in doing things on our own, in being independent, in relying on only ourselves. If we ask for help, others will see our brokenness, our need. It seems better to hide and suffer and muddle through alone than to open our lives to scrutiny and the possibility of criticism—and maybe change. We are so full of pride, even in our pain, that sometimes we think we might rather die than ask for help.

Forgive us; help us. We need other people around us, lifting us up, bearing our burdens, offering help and comfort. We need people who will speak hard, holy words with love. We need the warmth of others in this cold world. Help us, Lord, to let Your people in. Give us the courage to open our crossed arms, to look up and out toward others. Remind us that, from the beginning, we were designed for relationship. And our first relationship is with You. You are the Threefold God, the ultimate cord, never to be broken. Let us weave ourselves in—through prayer and meditation—to that eternal strand, where, strengthened by the Father, Son, and Holy Spirit, we will overcome. Amen.

Again, if two lie down together, then they have warmth; but how can one be warm alone? And though a man might prevail against him who is alone, two will withstand him. A threefold cord is not quickly broken.
ECCLESIASTES 4:11–12 AMPC

OPPRESSORS

$\mathcal{D}$ear Lord, so many people in the world are not free. They labor in terrible ways at another's bidding with no hope of escape. I pray for those in bondage—for freedom, safety, and justice. And in my small circle of influence, let me not be an oppressor as well. Let me not trample on the hearts or the bodies of Your precious people. Let me not walk in a way that wounds others, either deliberately or through inattention or preoccupation. I can be like an elephant, trampling others without even meaning to. I blunder in without listening, without thinking of anyone but myself. I want to be amusing and smart, and so I preen and posture, seeking admiration and affirmation.

Lord, forgive me. Turn my gaze off myself and on to others. I can't see others if I'm looking for my own reflection in their eyes. I praise You for giving me the example of Your Son, Jesus Christ, who though He was God in the flesh, threw off divinity to become a servant to us. He never forces; He asks. Let me seek only Your praise: "Well done, good and faithful servant." That will be enough. Amen.

In your relationships with one another, have the same mindset as Christ Jesus: Who, being in very nature God, did not consider equality with God something to be used to his own advantage; rather, he made himself nothing by taking the very nature of a servant.

PHILIPPIANS 2:5–7 NIV

Disastrous Kindness

*D*ear Father, You are kind and loving, but in holy hands those words can have the sharpest edge. I remember the Israelites wandered for forty years in the desert, and I think to myself, *That is a hard kindness.* You wanted them purified, and it took that long. When I suffer for even *four days*, I begin to doubt Your love and kindness. I moan and complain and sit in my self-pity instead of seeking You.

What are You saying to me in this, Lord? What would You have me learn? Show me my sin. Show me what is standing between us. Burn it away and draw me to Your side. I want Your refinement, and I want the love and kindness of a holy God—even when it cuts and burns. I want the protection of Your holiness. If I think I'll never commit certain sins, I'm a fool; I'm capable of anything. Only You can cleanse, only You can refine, only You allowed Your Son to be killed to save me. That is kindness; that is love. Lord, love me; be kind to me. And if in Your loving-kindness You take me through the fire to burn away the dross, I will praise You. Amen.

"I will refine them like silver and test them like gold. They will call on my name and I will answer them; I will say, 'They are my people,' and they will say, 'The Lord is our God.'"
ZECHARIAH 13:9 NIV

ACTS OF KINDNESS

Lord Jesus, You came to earth to do the will of the Father and nothing more, but that doesn't mean You lived a life of austerity and want. You slept when You were tired, You feasted with friends. You enjoyed company as well as solitude. You both gave gifts and received them. You listened to the voice of the Father in every situation, and what He required of You was not always hard. Sometimes it was delightful; sometimes He asked You to sit and let Your feet be bathed in perfume.

Your purposes may seem beyond us sometimes, but the promise of the Holy Spirit is that He will be a counselor to us, to show us, if we ask, the mind of God. You say if we seek, we will find. We seek the mind of God. Why have You put us here, in the circumstances we are in? Why have You given us the experiences we have had—both agreeable and difficult? In light of that, what would You have us do? What should we pray for? Who should we minister to and how? But also, how should we rest today? What gifts from Your hands would You have us delight in right now? We praise You for asking us to give *and* receive. Amen.

"But seek his kingdom, and these things will be given to you as well. Do not be afraid, little flock, for your Father has been pleased to give you the kingdom."
LUKE 12:31–32 NIV

SOLID GROUND

*D*ear God, You brought the universe into being from nothing, and You hold it all together. You speak, and the earth trembles. You move, and the mountains quake. Now the plates of this broken, cracked world press against each other; they buckle and fold and grind. Like faint reverberations of Your approach, earthquakes rock and shatter the ground, and we are felled and frightened. How can the very ground beneath us bring doubt? How can we walk, not knowing if our feet will hold us up steady? Where do we turn when what is solid crumbles into dust?

This is what Your Word says we should do: Go to the Rock that is higher. Set our feet on the Stone the builders rejected. Build our lives on the firm Foundation. We praise You that You are all those things—rock, stone, foundation—and more. Storms will come. The earth will move. Waves will wash over our heads. The earth, after all, is passing away, and it has been in its last days for two millennia. We pray for protection, also knowing that if our lives are built on the Solid Rock, we will not be shaken, no matter how the ground beneath us roils and churns. Amen.

"And the rain fell, and the floods came, and the winds blew and slammed against that house; and yet it did not fall, for it had been founded on the rock."
MATTHEW 7:25 NASB

All Things New

*D*ear Father, I think of Your kindness primarily as blessings: a job, a new baby, marriage, success, a comfortable home, plenty. And those are blessings for which I praise You. But sometimes—and my heart quails to pray this—the worst thing in the world is also Your kindness. Sometimes sickness, death, or failure are gifts from Your hands too. I recoil at such gifts, even though I know Your Word says Your plans are to prosper and not to harm me. How could those terrible things be good? How could they be Your plan? How could I be prospering in such circumstances?

But You speak to me gently, Lord, and say that when my sin, weakness, and emptiness are exposed, when I can no longer pretend to be okay, You can move in my life. When I see no way forward, that's when You will part the waters at my feet. When I have reached the utter end of myself—and I know this to be true—that's where You meet me. I realize I am nothing, I have nothing, and there is no hope apart from You, Jesus. At the end of *me*, I come to the beginning of *You*, which is the place where all things can be made new. Amen.

"For I know the plans I have for you," declares the
LORD, "plans to prosper you and not to harm you,
plans to give you hope and a future."
JEREMIAH 29:11 NIV

Different Gifts

*D*ear Lord, I caught myself silently criticizing the heart of another believer who was ministering to the sick but complaining. I was thinking I would have given that gift in a different spirit, with joy and willingness. Forgive me for my hypocrisy. The truth is I was *not* giving at all, not even in the ways I could have. I could have given encouragement to that believer. I could have prayed for the burden she was under. I give grudgingly also, just in different circumstances. Some things are easy for me to give away; other things my hands itch to hold on to.

Lord, help me to be thankful that the church is full of people with so many different gifts and generosities in so many different areas instead of criticizing what and how they give. Thank You that some can give time, some treasure, some wisdom, some help, some prayer. Thank You that members of the body are giving silently in ways nobody else has thought of. I pray You will encourage them. Enlarge our hearts to see and respond to the hurting, the needy—and those who are giving—in ways we never thought we could. All through Your grace, poured out on us, amen.

Every good gift and every perfect gift is from above, and cometh down from the Father of lights, with whom is no variableness, neither shadow of turning.
JAMES 1:17 KJV

Forgive to the Uttermost

*Y*our kindness, Lord, is to forgive and forgive and forgive. We wonder, sometimes, if we have reached the limits of Your kindness. We sin again and again in ways too numerous to list. We sin instantly, with just the lightest nudge of the world or adversity or pride. We sin in the same old ways, running in our devilish ruts over and over. Yet You know us so fully. You made us, and our sin does not surprise You. You know we are weak creatures, made of dust. You sit enthroned in heaven, wrapped in eternity as if it were a mantle, while we are born and die. We fade like the grass and disappear from the earth as though we never existed.

But You do not forget us. You always keep us in mind. And You provided a way out from under this burden of sin, through the perfect sacrifice of Your Son, Jesus Christ. His blood washes away our sin and carries it as far from us as the east is from the west. He reaches down and lifts us to Your side and into eternity. We praise You, Lord, for Your ocean of forgiveness and the unending gift of salvation. Amen.

For his unfailing love toward those who fear him is as great as the height of the heavens above the earth. He has removed our sins as far from us as the east is from the west.
PSALM 103:11–12 NLT

GOD REMEMBERS US

*D*ear Lord, often we race through our days trying to accomplish enough so death won't erase our legacy. We're terrified of being forgotten, of being, in the grand scheme of things, unremarkable. We want to earn a mention in the encyclopedia of life—if not a full article, then at least a footnote or two. But how many of us, no matter how hard we strive, will last longer in anyone's memory than a few generations? And in our selfish striving, how much are we missing of what You have for us? Simple pleasures, long conversations, meaningful relationships—these take time and energy but do little to pad our résumés.

Lord, show us Your heart in this matter. You say the things of this earth we call treasures are fleeting and fragile. They will be eaten by moths, riddled with rust, or carried off by thieves. They will not survive the grave; therefore, they are counterfeit treasures. Help us strive for what will last into eternity. Give us the willingness to be forgotten here while we store up treasures to be enjoyed with You forever. Amen.

"Do not lay up for yourselves treasures on earth, where moth and rust destroy and where thieves break in and steal, but lay up for yourselves treasures in heaven. . . . For where your treasure is, there your heart will be also."
MATTHEW 6:19–21 ESV

Truth Is Kindness

*D*ear Lord, I feel convicted about confronting the sin in another believer's life, but I'm balking at the responsibility. Who am I to tell them what to do? I'm just as sinful. Who am I to be Your agent for change? I struggle daily to do what You've called me to do. I'm sure I will meet only high walls of resistance and anger, so it seems easier and kinder to let their sin slide and preserve our relationship.

But You have no interest in ease and kindness where sin is concerned. Though You are infinitely patient with our sin, You never pretend it doesn't exist; You never ignore it or sweep it under the rug as we often do. You're not afraid to look sinful acts in the face and call them by name. Give me boldness, Lord, to speak what You have put on my heart. Give me Your confidence and grace. Remind me that I can't control the way people receive the message of the Gospel, only how faithfully and lovingly I deliver it. I pray that You will prepare the heart of this person whom You love, to hear what You have to say through me. Help me speak only what You would have me speak. Amen.

Rather, speaking the truth in love, we are to grow up
in every way into him who is the head, into Christ.
EPHESIANS 4:15 ESV

THE WAY

*L*ord, Your infinite kindness keeps us all from hell. We can do nothing to save ourselves, but You made a way for us through the sacrificial death of Your perfect Son. We can do nothing to deserve that sacrifice; we can only thank You for it. And we do. Thank You, thank You, Father. Thank You, Jesus, for being willing to die for us.

This world is full to overflowing with sin—just as in the days of Noah, just as it was in Sodom and Gomorrah. Some people think we're getting better and better all the time; they think we can build Your kingdom here without You. But all our righteousness is just filthy rags. Who can build the kingdom but the King? We can prepare our hearts for Your coming, but only You can annihilate sin. Sickness, poverty, war, injustice, fear, despair, murder, hate, and corruption will all flee when You come to reign. For where You are, sin cannot exist. You could have declared that You had had enough of us, that we had trespassed on Your kindness and patience long enough. You would have been perfectly justified in destroying us. But You didn't. You made a way where no way existed. And Jesus Christ our Lord is the way, the truth, and the life. All praise to Him. Amen.

"There is salvation in no one else! God has given no other name under heaven by which we must be saved."

ACTS 4:12 NLT

SECTION 6: *Goodness*

THE GOOD, GOOD FATHER

*L*ord, You are a good, good Father. You are *our* Father. We praise and thank You for buying us out of our slavery to sin and adopting us into Your family. You say we can call You Abba. That name is intimate and personal; it means "Daddy." But to many of us, the word *father* carries a terrible burden of association. We've had fathers who were absent or neglectful, who with their actions told us we were not important. We've had fathers who criticized us, who told us we had nothing of value to offer. We've even had fathers who abused us, who told us we were worth nothing.

We have listened to those lies, Lord, and sometimes we have believed that You, our heavenly Father, are saying the same things to us. We ask forgiveness for believing lies about You. We ask for Your grace to be able to forgive the fallible, earthly fathers who hurt us so deeply. We ask that Your transforming power will work in their hearts and bring repentance, reconciliation, and redemption. Lord, we ask that You will replace our faulty images of You with the truth: we have been chosen, we have been adopted, and we have nothing, ever, to fear. Amen.

For you did not receive the spirit of bondage again
to fear, but you received the Spirit of adoption
by whom we cry out, "Abba, Father."
ROMANS 8:15 NKJV

The Goodness of the Lord

*L*ord, I believe You are good, but I see so much evil around me. I believe You are loving, but I see so much hate. I believe You are just, but the wicked seem to carry on without hindrance. I believe Your promises are true, but these verses seem to promise something I don't understand.

What is Your goodness, Lord? Is it peace, prosperity, and a just society, things we can experience now? Or is it something different? Maybe what You're saying is that looking upon Your goodness in this life simply means *knowing You.* You promise to be as real to me as anything I can touch. And where is the land of the living? Just a few psalms before, You say we live in the valley of the shadow of death, not life. Though we are alive now, the land of the living, where there is no death, is yet to come. These beautiful promises are both already fulfilled and, somehow, still waiting to be fulfilled. They are true now, but they are just a shadow of what is to come. We praise You for being both knowable and beyond all comprehension. Who is like You? Amen.

I believe that I shall look upon the goodness of the LORD in the land of the living! Wait for the LORD; be strong, and let your heart take courage; wait for the LORD!
PSALM 27:13–14 ESV

Another Day to Do Good

*L*ord, I'm weary today. I've been busy with the tasks You set before me: leading, molding, modeling, admonishing, encouraging the people You have put in my care. I've been busy with the monotonous tasks of daily life: cleaning, organizing, cooking, shopping. They are all worthy of doing, and I am blessed to have the health, the means, and the time to accomplish them. I'm so thankful for where You have put me, Lord. But I can feel my spiritual tanks running empty, and I am thankful to escape for a few minutes to be alone and pray to You.

I need You every hour, most gracious Lord, to fill my cup again as I am being poured out in Your service. Let me not be weary in doing good, though what I do often seems both invisible and unimportant. You see me, and my quiet service gladdens Your heart. I am so thankful that You are a God who sees. You saw Hagar, pregnant and abandoned by the side of the road, and You see me now. Please strengthen me for the tasks You have ahead of me. I know my strength is Your strength working through me. Amen.

Let us not become weary in doing good, for at the proper time we will reap a harvest if we do not give up. Therefore, as we have opportunity, let us do good to all people.
Galatians 6:9–10 niv

Now Is the Day of Salvation

*D*ear Lord, I find myself trying to "protect" shallow relationships—with neighbors, acquaintances, relatives—by waiting to share the Gospel. I think a better time will come later or that maybe our relationships will deepen and I'll feel more comfortable sharing Your message of hope. But I know the time is *now*. How many days do I have left before it's too late to speak? Only You know. Fear in me is what makes me think the Gospel will—at some point in the future—become more palatable. No matter how I try to polish it up, or add bows and ribbons, the Gospel stands unchanged. It is unique in time and space. Jesus, who is God, became a man and, because of His great love, took the punishment we deserved for our sins. He declares us righteous in His eyes when we believe in Him.

Forgive me for my cowardice, Lord, and help me to trust that without You there is *no good thing*. Help me to hope in You for others and nothing else. Not a better time or location. Not better words or a more-clever angle. Just the simple Gospel, which is the power of God for salvation. Amen.

For he says, "In the time of my favor I heard you, and in the day of salvation I helped you." I tell you, now is the time of God's favor, now is the day of salvation.
2 Corinthians 6:2 niv

Who Is Our Titus?

*D*ear Lord, we are not okay. We have conflict within us, and conflict without. Inside, where no one can see, are doubt, bitterness, anger, selfishness, judgment, and anxiety. Outside, visible to all, are the harsh words and unjust actions that give rise to all the evil in the world. That sin is like a giant boulder, gathering speed as it rolls out from our hearts, crushing everyone in its path.

But this is the state of our fallen world. You, Lord, do not call us to perfection in our own strength, but to partake of the perfection only Your Son provides. It's okay not to be okay. But You are so gracious to us. Though we are broken within and constant contributors to the brokenness without, You don't leave us there. Just as Paul and Timothy and the believers in Macedonia were encouraged by the arrival of Titus, so You provide encouragers for us, if only we have the eyes to see them. Books, hymns, other believers, and Your timeless Word can all be used by the Spirit to sustain us when we are weak. Give us eyes and ears open to how You are encouraging us, Lord. And let us be ready and eager to encourage others. In Your name, Amen.

We faced conflict from every direction, with battles on the outside and fear on the inside. But God, who encourages those who are discouraged, encouraged us by the arrival of Titus.
2 Corinthians 7:5–6 NLT

The Plains of Sodom

Dear Father, You call me to be holy and set apart, but sometimes I find myself creeping closer to what, even if it isn't inherently sinful, could become sin to me. A relationship, a habit, a curiosity. They aren't wrong, but suddenly I find myself facing the wrong direction. I don't want to be like Lot. I don't want to pitch my tents close to Sodom, even though the land is beautiful, well-watered, and Edenic. Lot was weak, as I am, and his choice eventually cost him everything he had. He escaped with the clothes on his back as fire and brimstone fell around him. From a safe distance, I can say I want to be holy, but I need the wisdom of Your Spirit to show me how I'm courting evil while still imagining I'm keeping myself separate.

Help me not to be like Lot, living as close to sin and compromise as I dare. Help me instead to live as close to You as I can. Help me seek holiness. Help me, Lord, to be willing to look at my life and not excuse or wink at my sin. Help me to see my sin as You see it, and to hate it. In Your holy, precious name, amen.

"All the land that you see I will give to you and your offspring forever. . . . Go, walk through the length and breadth of the land, for I am giving it to you."
Genesis 13:15, 17 niv

Contentment

*D*ear Lord, I'm struggling with material desires that just seem to grow. When I read magazines, watch television, or wander on the internet, I see things I never knew existed, and suddenly my life seems incomplete without them. I want them, and my mind begins to scheme to get them. Contentment is gone, and I think it will return only when I hold the precious, wanted objects in my hands.

Lord, I confess this and ask for Your help. I don't want my peace and contentment held hostage to every wind of desire. My hope is in You, not the things of this world, because even when they are brand-new in their boxes and wrappers, they are already fading away. You have given me everything I really need. I have been showered with blessings; I want for nothing. Remind me when I feel the pull of "new things," to count Your blessings, to name them one by one. Help me rehearse— even to speak aloud—what You have done for me. And I know You're not finished blessing me. You are generous beyond anything I deserve, and You delight in giving to me. Thank You for the peace of resting in Your provision. Amen.

But godliness with contentment is great gain.
For we brought nothing into this world, and it is
certain we can carry nothing out. And having
food and raiment let us be therewith content.
1 TIMOTHY 6:6–8 KJV

For the Innocent

*D*ear Lord, this world—though it has moments of beauty and goodness—is fractured with injustice. People whose only crime was being at the wrong place at the wrong time languish behind bars. Justice often wars with bureaucracy, and those without resources or advocates are crushed in the clash. We pray for those who are unjustly accused. Give them hope and strength to continue fighting for their freedom. Raise up warriors for justice, people who are willing to fight a broken system. So often we want to believe people must be guilty as charged; it's too painful to believe in their innocence. We might have to speak up. We might have to act. We might become enmeshed in the struggle in ways that could put us or our loved ones in danger.

But we serve a Savior who was unjustly accused. He was beaten, mocked, and executed although He committed no crime. Jesus lived and died to give hope to the hopeless captives, to remind them a day of judgment and justice is coming, when all wrongs will be righted. Perfect peace will reign for the first time since creation. We wait and pray for that day. Let it come quickly. Amen.

Powerful is your arm! Strong is your hand! Your right hand is lifted high in glorious strength. Righteousness and justice are the foundation of your throne. Unfailing love and truth walk before you as attendants.

Psalm 89:13–14 nlt

WHO STANDS FOR US?

*L*ord, I find anxiety creeping into my soul again like a chilly fog. I thought a long spell of regularly drinking in Your Word had banished it. I thought it was gone for good. I'm scared of how it makes me feel: alone, untethered, dizzy. I know anxiety is a lie, a glimpse of a godless world I need to immediately repudiate. The Devil is the one saying to me that You do not exist, that You are not in control, that I'm on my own in a universe that does not have me in mind.

Thank You for reminding me there is no point of stasis in this life. We are always either moving toward or away from You. The fight for our souls will never be over until the day we hear You say, "Well done, good and faithful servant." That truth can either crush us—if we think we're waging this war in our own strength—or give us incredible hope and comfort. We are not alone in this fight. You stand ready to rush in at any moment and intercede for us. You stand at the right hand of the Father doing just that. Thank You for Your constant, abiding love. Amen.

Who then is the one who condemns? No one. Christ Jesus who died—more than that, who was raised to life— is at the right hand of God and is also interceding for us.

ROMANS 8:34 NIV

Here and Now

$\mathscr{D}$ear Lord, I find myself looking forward to an imagined future when life will be easier. Children will be older and less needy, my garden will have fewer weeds, the weather will be warmer and sunnier, I'll have more time to cultivate the relationships I cherish most.

When I'm seeing most clearly, however, I realize I'm giving the future a power only You possess. It can't give me strength to get through trying days; it doesn't give me hope. And in focusing on what is to come, I'm sacrificing the present to the idol of the future. Forgive me. I know You want me to be present in this moment because it's all I have right now. The future—though You hold it in Your hands—is unknown to me. I cannot live in its faint light, save for the sure knowledge of my future in heaven with You. You tell me to pray for the things of *this day*—daily bread, present sins and temptations, protection. I lift those up to You. Thank You for where You have placed me and for what I am walking through right now. I know You are here with me. Amen.

Give us this day our daily bread. And forgive us our debts, as we forgive our debtors. And lead us not into temptation, but deliver us from evil: For thine is the kingdom, and the power, and the glory, for ever. Amen.
MATTHEW 6:11–13 KJV

Let God Be God

*D*ear Lord, I'm wrestling with anger and disappointment. Someone close to me is making terrible choices that are affecting everyone around her. I want instant change, Lord! I want her to grow up! I want her to acknowledge that I'm right and she's wrong. But I know pride is infusing my attitude. I want change where *I* think it is needed, and I want it on *my* timetable. You want change too, but I quail at the thought that the change You desire most may be in *me*.

Forgive me for my anger, my impatience, my lack of trust, my desire to control every situation. I cannot be the savior of anyone, not even me—and to think I can is to say, like Satan did, that I can be like God. I pray You will work in her life and that I'll allow You to do Your work in Your own way. Show me what You want me to do. But my heart is hurting. Please comfort me. Where is Your goodness in this? I don't pray this with doubt, Lord; I pray it with expectation. Your goodness *is* in this situation, even if I can't see it yet. In faith and hope, amen.

Why, my soul, are you downcast? Why so disturbed
within me? Put your hope in God, for I will
yet praise him, my Savior and my God.

PSALM 42:5 NIV

Pause to Praise

Lord, our lists of wants never seem to shrink. Until we see You in glory and are fully satisfied, they probably never will. But it's good to practice the discipline of turning our hearts to praise.

We praise You today for being both the God of our fathers and the God of our children: unchanging, eternal. We praise You that we don't need to reinterpret You for each succeeding generation; You are true in every time and place. We praise You that You are perfect and holy—not a trickster god, but the One who can be counted upon always. We praise You that You are light, and that You allow us to see. Though fallen and fading, our bodies remind us to praise You for the body of Your Son, broken and poured out for us. And the fact that we are daily wasting away reminds us to praise You for how Your Spirit renews us inwardly. Let our struggles become reminders of Your faithfulness. Let our failures be reminders of Your goodness. Let our afflictions be reminders of eternity. Everything can be turned to praise. Lord, Your goodness is beyond imagining, and we praise You. Let everything that has breath praise You. Amen.

Men shall speak of the might of Your awesome acts, and I will declare Your greatness. They shall utter the memory of Your great goodness, and shall sing of Your righteousness.
PSALM 145:6–7 NKJV

By Quiet Waters

*L*ord, I followed a stream in the woods today to where it emptied into a salt marsh. In the distance, the ocean glittered. You were there. You were there in the quiet sounds of water running over rocks. You were there in the cushions of bright green moss on the forest floor. You were there in the intricate whorls of lichen on the birch trees. You were there in the gentle gray sky. And You were there in the voices of my companions: a baby who toddled along, burbling as sweetly as the brook, and a little girl who skipped along the path like a goat.

Thank You for the world and the things and the people in it. So often I rush through my days without stopping to notice and thank You for the many loving details You stitched into the fabric of creation. It is fearfully and wonderfully made, just as I am. Thank You for helping me stop and look and *enjoy* what You've given me. Thank You for the peace that comes from being fully present in the moment. Please help me bring the outside in, so I can learn to live more fully in the peace Your presence gives. Amen.

There is a river whose streams make glad the city of God, the holy dwelling places of the Most High. God is in the midst of her, she will not be moved.
Psalm 46:4–5 nasb

WRITTEN ON STONE

$\mathcal{D}$ear Father, please protect the goodness of the Sabbath in my life. I feel the world encroaching and pushing and arguing that Sunday is just like any other day, to use as I please. It says that to keep Sunday distinct from the other days of the week—set apart, holy—is to be legalistic and rigid. In a world where busyness is a measure of one's importance, resting seems suspect. I admit, Lord, that my thoughts drift that way too. Instead of thinking how I can please and honor You by keeping the Sabbath holy, I think about how much I can get away with doing on Sunday.

Forgive me for this creeping disobedience. Help me to look different from other people in the way I live this day. You gave us ten rules to live by. We understand instinctively that murder, lying, stealing, and adultery are wrong. We understand that we must not worship idols or profane Your holy name. We understand the wisdom and justice of honoring our parents. The fourth commandment, however, is the one we are all too ready to discard. But it was important enough to You to carve it on stone. Help me trust Your wisdom and guidance, Father, and honor the Sabbath by keeping it holy. Amen.

> *"For in six days the* Lord *made the heavens*
> *and the earth, the sea, and all that is in them,*
> *and rested the seventh day. Therefore the* Lord
> *blessed the Sabbath day and hallowed it."*
> Exodus 20:11 NKJV

LIFE OF PRAISE

*D*ear Lord, You ask us to live a life of praise, to lift our hands and sing Your praises. This is against our nature. Left to our own devices, we would live a life of self-satisfaction; we would praise each other and ourselves; we would worship things that are about the same size as ourselves, because then we would be gods; and we would serve ourselves first at the banquet of life. But Your miracle in us is that we no longer live enslaved to our old nature. We are new creations, and we praise You for this supernatural re-creation. We could do nothing to bring it about; it is an act of Your Spirit.

But, Lord, the old man—or woman or child—continually rears up, wanting to take over again. We ask You to fill us daily with the Spirit that is the source of our newness in Christ. We need to be made new daily, hourly. Praise is an integral part of this new life. With it, we choose to undergo a constant reorienting to Your goodness. We ask that You continually remind and enable us to "turn our eyes upon Jesus and look full in His wonderful face." Amen.

Therefore, if anyone is in Christ, the new creation has come: The old has gone, the new is here! All this is from God, who reconciled us to himself through Christ.
2 CORINTHIANS 5:17–18 NIV

Not the End

*D*ear Father, this world is full of death, and it scares us. Death was not part of Your original plan. You created us for eternal life in a garden. But because of the sin of our long-ago parents, echoing through the centuries, we have death and thorns instead. Death and the curse of the ground have no part of Your eternal, life-giving nature, and perhaps that's why they seem so wrong to us, who were created in Your image.

We thank You that the strangeness of death gives us a hint of our eternal soul and points us to You. We thank You for the glimpses of our eternal home in Your Word. We will see mansions, streets of gold, streams, trees, fruit, and a heavenly city, but what it will look like and what we will do there exactly are beyond words. Heaven is more than we could ever describe or imagine. Help us look forward to that day with anticipation, not dread. We don't need to fear, because we know You are good, and that death is not the end. We don't know exactly what is on the other side of death's high wall, but we know *who* is there. That is enough. Amen.

For we know that if our earthly house, this tent,
is destroyed, we have a building from God, a house
not made with hands, eternal in the heavens.
2 Corinthians 5:1 nkjv

THE GOODNESS OF THE GIVER

*L*ord, I am in the world, but not of the world. I have a mortal body, but an immortal soul. I am born again through Your Spirit, but I sin. I believe with all my heart, but I don't know for certain. This dual nature is difficult, and I find myself swinging between extremes. Some days I'm a hedonist: I swim in the pleasures and joys of this life without thinking much about who has given them to me. Other days, I am an ascetic who uses self-denial to feel more spiritual. This double-mindedness produces anxiety and grief because one extreme is hollow and the other is unsustainable. On my own, I cannot navigate the chasm between body and spirit. Jesus alone can bridge that gap.

I praise You that Jesus both fasted and feasted. I praise You that He could revel in the delight of perfumed oil rubbed into His bare feet and that He could also bear the nails driven through the skin and bones of those same feet. He could enjoy Your gifts without losing sight of the Giver. He knew the perfect joy of continual thanksgiving. I ask You for that, Lord. Let me enjoy Your gifts—and let my heart overflow with praise and thanks. Amen.

And the Word became flesh and dwelt among us,
and we have seen his glory, glory as of the only
Son from the Father, full of grace and truth.
JOHN 1:14 ESV

Speaking of God's Goodness

$\mathcal{D}$ear Lord, my fear of being an ineffective evangelist often seals my lips before I've even spoken a word. I'm afraid I won't know what to say, that I will stumble or sound stupid, that I'll be asked questions I don't know how to answer. I confess these fears, Lord, and ask for Your forgiveness. I also confess the sin at the root of my fears: thinking You are not enough.

Again, forgive me. I know You are sufficient for me, and that means You are also sufficient for every unbeliever who has ever denied Your existence or power. Help me prepare thoughtfully for evangelism by reading, praying, and practicing. But also, help me depend on You; the promise that Your Spirit will speak through us is not a promise made only to the Billy Grahams, Lee Strobels, and Ravi Zachariases of this world. That promise is for every believer. You will give me words, you will give me answers, and if I stumble, You will use even that. Your Word says You use the foolish to shame the wise. Let me be willing to sound like a fool as I speak of Your goodness to those around me. Amen.

"God will give you the right words at the right time. For it is not you who will be speaking—it will be the Spirit of your Father speaking through you."
Matthew 10:19–20 nlt

SECTION 7: *Faithfulness*

EVIDENCE SEEN

*D*ear Lord, thank You that we can believe in the unseen and know beyond a shadow of a doubt that it is real. We praise You for the firm conviction that things not seen are just as true, just as firm, just as sure. Faith is not a crutch for a weak mind, but the conviction of a mind, fully awake, allowed by the Spirit of the living God to see beyond what can be touched to the eternal reality that undergirds, upholds, and explains it.

What is this world without You, Lord? It would be beauty without reason, it would be motion without purpose, it would be symmetry and story that turn out to be only accident. That would be intolerable and lead to despair, which is the silent cry of the world today. Help us to be the invisible made visible, to be the evidence *seen* by the hurting world. Our lives—transformed, made new, redeemed—may be the only evidence many people see of the truth of the Gospel of Jesus Christ. Be real in our lives, Lord, and draw others to that reality. Praise to the Savior who makes and will make all things new. Amen.

Now faith is the substance of things hoped for, the evidence of things not seen. . . . Through faith we understand that the worlds were framed by the word of God, so that things which are seen were not made of things which do appear.
HEBREWS 11:1, 3 KJV

STANDING ON THE PROMISES

*D*ear Father, promises made to us have been broken, and we have broken promises to others in return. We have grieved, and we have caused grief for others. Forgive us for our faithlessness, our inconstancy, our selfishness. But You, Lord, are faithful to every word You utter. You have never made an empty promise; if a promise You made has not already been fulfilled, it will be soon, as surely as the dawn is coming.

We praise You that Your Word is truth and that no promise will be left undone. We praise You for promising a hope and a future to childless Abraham—and then giving him Isaac. We praise You for promising a deliverer to your enslaved people—and then sending Moses. We praise You for promising Adam and Eve that one of their offspring would crush the head of Satan—and then sending Jesus. And we praise You, Father, for promising to send Jesus again to make all things new. We wait and hope for that day, knowing that He who promises is faithful. Help us to stand on Your promises in these dark days, through fear, grief, and suffering. Give us a renewed faithfulness, both to You and to the people around us. Amen.

> *"God is not human, that he should lie,*
> *not a human being, that he should change*
> *his mind. Does he speak and then not act?"*
> NUMBERS 23:19 NIV

WHEN PERSECUTION COMES

*D*ear Lord, I see believers in other countries martyred for their faith, killed for speaking Your name or for refusing to recant the truth. Others are jailed, beaten, or have their livelihoods ruined. Still others are disowned by their families. I lift those faithful believers to You right now. Comfort and sustain them, Lord. Be present in their suffering; be glorified in their lives and witness.

I have never suffered for Your name, at least in such obvious ways. But I've been thought a fool, and friends I loved have turned away. Yet You promise us two things: in this world we will have trouble and You have overcome the world. These truths are scary and heartening at the same time. The world is gearing up for a final battle; the players are moving into place. Persecution will come, and my prayer is that I will be found faithful. Help me hold fast to You no matter what comes my way—fire, nakedness, danger, sword, or simply ridicule. I am full of fear, and I need Your strength. I thank You that Your strength and wisdom are mine for the asking and that my part is just to hold fast to the confession of my hope without wavering, because You have promised to be with me. And You are faithful. Amen.

Let us hold fast the confession of our hope without wavering, for He who promised is faithful.
HEBREWS 10:23 NKJV

GREAT IS YOUR FAITHFULNESS

*L*ord, You have shown me lately the depth of my unfaithfulness. My love for difficult people has grown cold, and I have rejected the promise that You are working all things together for good. I have indulged in sinful thoughts and wished ill on the people making life difficult for me. I have longed for ease over sanctification. I have been willing to love only when it is convenient or when I get the right response in return.

But that is not the kind of love to which You have called me. Lord, forgive me. Change my cold heart to a heart of flesh. I know it's only through Your Spirit and the love Jesus showed to *me* on the cross that I can love in return. I ask You to fill me with that kind of love. It's unnatural love, supernatural love, a love I could never summon in my own power. But it is the only kind of love You give. It's a love that burns away our sin, yet does not consume us. It's a love that sees every fault, yet never fails in compassion. It's a love as large every morning as it was the day before. It's a love that stretches from creation into eternity without flinching. Great is Your faithfulness. Amen!

Because of the LORD's great love we are not consumed, for his compassions never fail. They are new every morning; great is your faithfulness.
LAMENTATIONS 3:22–23 NIV

Rooted

*D*ear Lord, in this country, the days when most people lived and died within a few miles of where they were born are long past. Today we can fly to the other side of the world in a day; we can get into a car and drive five hundred miles in any direction without worrying about packing provisions or finding ourselves in completely unknown territory. We have maps, credit cards, gas stations, and endless miles of smooth, safe roads.

But with that incredible freedom has come a certain rootlessness. We admit our tendency to think the grass is greener in some other place. We admit we are often unwilling to bear the burden of staying put, the burden of discipline, obedience, sacrifice, and faithfulness. When things get hard—and they always will—we want to run away, not stay and be conformed to Your image. But You are a God faithful to a place and a people. Give us that faithfulness to the places, people, and churches among whom You have settled us. Rooted in You, we know we will grow wherever You plant us. And when You lead us to travel or move, we ask that You will be our pillar of fire and cloud. Amen.

. . .that you, being rooted and grounded in love,
may be able to comprehend with all the saints what
is the breadth and length and height and depth, and
to know the love of Christ which surpasses knowledge.
Ephesians 3:17–19 nasb

Smash Our Idols

*D*ear Lord, we desire many things. Are You among them? We want the stuff of this world: nice houses, delicious foods, new cars, stylish clothes, the devices and trinkets of each passing season. We desire peace and prosperity and blessings. Wanting these things is not wrong; they are all gifts from Your hand. But do we desire You—the giver—with the same fervency? Do we desire You, Lord, or just what You give us? Do we seek Your wonderful face, or do we look past You to the next new thing?

Lord, we ask You today to search our hearts and reveal the wicked, idolatrous ways in us. We can make an idol out of anything, and we do. We ask You to smash them, no matter how painful that is for us, because we want You more than anything else. It's easy to say that without really meaning it, however. So we also pray that our Savior will be interceding for us by Your throne; we pray that Your Spirit will fill us and displace everything not of You. Let the things of this world grow dim, until You are our all in all. Amen.

> *"If you want to return to the LORD with all your hearts, get rid of your foreign gods and your images of Ashtoreth. Turn your hearts to the LORD and obey him alone; then he will rescue you."*
>
> 1 SAMUEL 7:3 NLT

ANOTHER YEAR

*D*ear Father, I thank You for a new year and another birthday to remind me that I'm growing older—as if the crow's-feet and silver hairs I see in the mirror aren't reminder enough. I'm growing nearer to the day when my life on this earth will end. Some days I am glad of that, and some days I want to hold on to this life and its joys as long as possible.

Lord, help me number my days aright so I may gain a heart of wisdom. My gray hairs mean nothing by themselves; they are only something to celebrate if they represent years spent drawing closer to You. But I don't want to be foolish as I age. I crave that heart of wisdom. I want to be able to weather storms; I long to be rooted deep in You and to be watered by the living water that never runs dry. Make my wrinkles mean something; make them marks of a life lived in Your service and for Your glory, to the very end. I truly believe evil, sickness, sin, and corruption—both in me and in the world—will be defeated, and I will enter glory to the sound of trumpets proclaiming Your final triumph. Amen.

When the perishable has been clothed with the imperishable, and the mortal with immortality, then the saying that is written will come true: "Death has been swallowed up in victory."

1 CORINTHIANS 15:54 NIV

We May Not See the Day

*D*ear Father, Your apostles, disciples, and followers in the early church expected to see You return at any moment. They said, "Be ready! Be watchful!" But You didn't come. Centuries have passed, and people continue to say Your coming is just around the corner. They name a date and cite evidence for their belief. But the date passes, every time, and You don't come.

Forgive them for their presumption; only You know the day and hour of Jesus' return. Even the angels in heaven are waiting, just as we are. I look at the sky when I see clouds gathering at sunset, and I listen for that trumpet, straining my ears. But all I hear is silence. Lord, it's hard to hold on to the belief that You're coming soon when the days begin and end as they have, over and over, for thousands of years. I begin to lose faith that the day is drawing nigh when You will dwell with us and everything broken will be made new. Give me the faith to keep longing and praying for Your coming, even though I may not see it. Come, Lord Jesus, come. Amen.

Henceforth there is laid up for me the crown of righteousness, which the Lord, the righteous judge, will award to me on that day, and not only to me but also to all who have loved his appearing.
2 Timothy 4:8 esv

Catechism Questions

$\mathcal{D}$ear Lord, when I find myself full of doubts and questions, You remind me that You are the answer to all of them. Does evil threaten? You are my high tower. Am I weak and broken? You are my strength. Am I sick? You are the healer. Am I scared? You are the rock to which I can run. Am I discouraged? You are the lifter of my head. Is my sin more than I can bear? You have taken my every sin and clothed me in Your righteousness. Is hate everywhere I turn? You are love. Do I fear the future? You knew all the days ordained for me before one of them came to be. Do I feel lost? You left the ninety-nine to find me—and then You rejoiced when You did! Am I angry? You tell me to examine my own heart first. Am I grieving? You cried too. Do I rail at injustice? You see everything and will exact perfect justice at the proper time.

Remind me to come to You, Lord, even if I am broken by my fear and confusion. No matter how I stumble, waver, and wander, Your truth is always the same. It's the one fixed point. Teach me to preach the Gospel to myself daily, hourly, in every minute. In praise of Your faithfulness, amen.

> *"For God so loved the world, that he gave his only Son, that whoever believes in him should not perish but have eternal life."*
> JOHN 3:16 ESV

"Helping" God Along

*D*ear Lord, in Genesis 15 Abraham gets these amazing promises from You. You tell him he doesn't need to fear because You will be his shield and great reward. Though he is childless, You tell him his offspring will be as numerous as the stars. Though he is a wanderer with no settled home, You tell him You will give him possession of a fruitful land. You give him a startling vision as a covenant: *You*, Yourself, the sovereign Lord, pass between the halves of the sacrificial animals, saying to Abraham—and to us—that You will pay the price with Your own blood if that covenant is broken. Yet in the very next chapter, Abraham forgets that night of smoke and fire and the presence of God, and he seeks to hurry You along and fulfill the covenant himself, begetting a child with his maidservant, Hagar.

We are just like Abraham, Lord. We repeatedly forget Your promises, despite how they are laid out for us in Your Word, despite the sacrifice of Jesus, who fulfilled the covenant when we could not, and despite the Spirit who lives in us as a guarantee of those promises. Show us the subtle ways we doubt Your promises and try to "help" You along. Amen.

When the sun had set and darkness had fallen,
a smoking firepot with a blazing torch appeared
and passed between the pieces. On that day
the Lord made a covenant with Abram.
Genesis 15:17–18 niv

KICKING AND SCREAMING

*W*e live like the people of Sodom, Lord: we flaunt perversion and call it freedom. We worship the creation rather than the One who created it. We think our sins are marks of sophistication. We delight in our own images and forget in whose image we were made. Forgive us. We know our sins deserve condemnation; we too deserve the fire and brimstone that rained down on Sodom. Scoffers may laugh, as some did then, but their laughter will turn to dust and ashes in their mouths on the day of judgment.

But amid that fearful judgment, look at Lot! Though warned, he lingered and hesitated until You led him out by the hand. It sounds like You *pulled* him! That is love; that is faithfulness. To him and to us. And the saying is true: there but for the grace of God go I. But for Your restraining, saving, grasping hand, we would be condemned. We would choose Sodom over heaven; we would choose to stay and burn rather than be rescued. Thank You for pulling us back from the brink. Thank You for our undeserved, unlooked-for salvation and the Savior who stood in the fire for us. All praise to the God who saves! Amen.

*But while he lingered, the men seized him and his
wife and his two daughters by the hand, for the
Lord was merciful to him; and they brought
him forth and set him outside the city.*
GENESIS 19:16 AMPC

Idols Overboard

*D*ear Lord, I long to smash the idols that have grown between us, but sometimes I don't even recognize them. All I see are habits, personality quirks, tendencies, and tastes, while You see false gods to which I am bowing without even realizing it.

I ask You to show me what I have propped up on Your altar. Show me my heart, Lord, and help me give back to You the parts of it that have been devoted to something or someone other than You. I long to return to You. But You are holy and righteous and altogether different; to my sinful heart, holiness feels like loss. Make me brave in stepping toward You and leaving behind what hinders me. Sometimes it feels like trying to walk on water. How will I stay afloat without those precious habits, personality quirks, tendencies, and tastes I think are holding me up? I long to be held up only by You, but I'm scared, Lord. You are the water under my feet. You are the air buffeting me. You are the hands reaching out to hold me. Give me the faith to step out of the boat and know I don't need solid ground under my feet. *You* are the only solid ground. Idols will sink, and You will bear me up. Amen.

> *"I will give them an undivided heart and put a*
> *new spirit in them; I will remove from them their*
> *heart of stone and give them a heart of flesh."*
> Ezekiel 11:19 niv

Faithful to All Generations

*D*ear Father, we praise You for Your long faithfulness to Your people. We praise You for clothing Adam and Eve and not destroying them. We praise You for the promises You made Abraham and then fulfilled. We praise You for protecting the baby Moses as he floated in the Nile. We praise You for bringing Your people out of slavery in Egypt. We praise You for protecting Rahab and her family. We praise You for bringing Your people home from captivity time and time again. We praise You for fulfilling Your promise to send the Messiah.

We praise You for preserving a remnant of Your people from the horrors of the Holocaust. We praise You for how You are spreading the message of salvation in this digital age so that very soon *all will have heard*. You are faithful to all generations. That means us too, not just the people in the Bible. Help us to remember and proclaim Your faithfulness in our lives so others will see and know that You are a loving, faithful God. And we look forward to the vantage point of heaven, where we will see with awe and wonder the vast scope of Your faithfulness in unbroken glory. Amen.

"Go home to your own people and tell them how much the Lord has done for you, and how he has had mercy on you." So the man went away and began to tell in the Decapolis how much Jesus had done for him.
MARK 5:19–20 NIV

All for Love

*D*ear Lord, I praise You today for the injustice You suffered for my sake. You, who are God, came to earth and took on a finite body. For the One who ranged the Milky Way, it was probably like living inside a burlap sack! You, who existed at the dawn of creation, slowed to the pedestrian pace of life in minutes and hours and years. You, the omnipresent God, walked along dusty roads or rode a plodding donkey. You, who enjoyed the perfect communion of the Trinity, spent three years teaching people who never quite understood Your message.

The God who is perfect in justice stood before a mocking crowd and was falsely accused. The Sinless One carried the weight of all the sins since that sweet, brief period of perfection in the garden. The Author of life was killed. When I feel sorry for myself, I think of You. When I despair for this unjust world, I remember You, Jesus, and what You endured. Your humanity brought me hope. Your punishment brought me peace. Your scars brought me healing. You carried my sins like they were Yours. It was all for love, and I can offer nothing in return but praise. Amen.

When he sees all that is accomplished by his anguish,
he will be satisfied. And because of his experience,
my righteous servant will make it possible for many
to be counted righteous, for he will bear all their sins.
Isaiah 53:11 nlt

Broken Yet Singing

*L*ord, we are broken and scarred and put back together crooked. We are hurting and confused. We are lost and scared, grasping at anything to survive. We are sheep without a shepherd—in a din of bleating and stumbling woolly backs. We desperately need a Savior. We need someone to lead us, guide us, comfort us, and heal us. We need You, Jesus. Though we know You, we are forever turning away. When life is easy, we think we're succeeding all on our own. When life is hard, we ignore You until the pain becomes too great to bear. It seems that running to You is never our first response, yet You are always there.

We thank You that we can't wander to any place where You can't reach us. We praise You that there is no sin You cannot forgive and redeem. We praise You that You are always standing at the door of our hearts, knocking, ready to enter, no matter how long we have ignored You or how many times we have invited You in only to push You out later. Who can fathom such infinite, patient love? Though we are broken beyond reason, because of You we can sing the song of the redeemed. Amen.

Wondrously show your steadfast love, O Savior of those who seek refuge from their adversaries at your right hand. Keep me as the apple of your eye; hide me in the shadow of your wings.
PSALM 17:7–8 ESV

INFINITE MERCY

*L*ord, You are infinitely creative. We see it in the complex dance of the planets and stars and in the endless variety of the flowers that dot our meadows and forests. We see it in the dazzling array of creatures that populate this earth. Our own miraculous bodies testify to Your precise and beautiful design. And no matter at what scale we view Your creation, it is magnificent—from galaxies and mountain ranges to snowflakes and molecules. There is beauty wherever we look.

We thank You too for the infinite forms Your mercy takes. It can be as quick as lightning, as patient as a glacier, as hard as a diamond, or as soft as a kiss. It can shout, or it can whisper. We know the mercy we see is only a part of the mercy You extend to us. Because You hold this world in Your loving hands, miracles we know nothing about happen, continually. We thank You for that infinite mercy, which overwhelms and drowns and obliterates the sin we are so good at creating. We are made in Your image, Lord, and we long to create beauty, goodness, and truth like You do. Enable us and fill us with Your Holy Spirit to that high calling. Amen.

*And the L*ORD *said, "I will cause all my goodness*
to pass in front of you, and I will proclaim my
*name, the L*ORD, *in your presence. I will have*
mercy on whom I will have mercy."
EXODUS 33:19 NIV

To the Ends of the Earth

*D*ear Father, I thank You today for the men and women who have given up comfort and safety to take the Gospel to people who have never heard of You. Thank You for those who travel to distant cities, nations, or tribes; for those who learn to speak new languages and live in unfamiliar cultures. I ask that You give them boldness to speak the name of Jesus and perseverance amid trials. I ask that Your Spirit go before them and move in the hearts of their listeners to receive the message of the Gospel. I ask that You provide for them financial assistance, materials, and helpers, and enable them to stand firm. You don't guarantee protection, but You promise that, of those You have called, none will be plucked out of Your hand.

Give them faithfulness, no matter if they are flooded with converts or never see the fruit from their labor in this life. And, Lord, I ask that You give them faith enough in *Your* faithfulness to be able to enjoy times of peace and refreshing, despite the work still left to be done. Amen.

"But you will receive power when the Holy Spirit has come upon you, and you will be my witnesses in Jerusalem and in all Judea and Samaria, and to the end of the earth."
Acts 1:8 esv

SECTION 8: *Gentleness*

THE STILL, SMALL VOICE

*L*ord, I praise You today for Your gentleness. You don't force or coerce belief. You don't trample on our free will. You don't pry open our hearts and insert Your Spirit like a shunt or stint, even if our souls are sick unto death. You don't convert at the edge of a sword, even though we sometimes try to force others to conversion. You are infinitely patient and gentle with Your creatures. You wait, You whisper, You comfort.

I long to be gentle like You, Lord. I want to wait, to listen, to heal with both my silence and my words. But so often my desire to speak, to *be comforted* myself, and to do things now wins out, and instead of acting like You, I act like me: angry, impatient, rough. Forgive me, Lord. I pray Your Spirit will so fill me that what overflows is You and not me. The amazing thing about You is that You stoop to fill us with Your nature. You don't hold Yourself far off and aloof. You come in. No other god is like You. You are a God who longs for His creatures to partake of His very self. Thank You that Your gentleness is not weakness, and Your quiet voice speaks only truth. Let us be like that. Amen.

> *For by these He has granted to us His precious and magnificent promises, so that by them you may become partakers of the divine nature.*
> 2 PETER 1:4 NASB

The Teeming World

Lord, this world is full and bursting at the seams. More people are alive today than have lived in all of history. The cities of the world teem with life—and the curses that can come with high population: pollution, crime, disease, and hunger. There is no utopia here; that waits for heaven. We don't see how the earth can continue to sustain us all, yet we know that to You, all life—small, large, unformed, aged, misshapen, comely, rich, poor—is precious.

Jesus, You ministered surrounded by needy, grasping crowds, but You didn't push them away, and You didn't ignore little hands pulling at You. You had compassion on them. They were like sheep without a shepherd, You said. When we think of the world and its billions, do we think of people as Your sheep? Do we think in terms of harvest? Each person is a soul poised before heaven or hell. Lord, let us be willing to be moved with compassion. Let us be willing to be crowded, jostled, pushed, and inconvenienced. Let us be willing to endure the noise, smell, and confusion of the unsaved. Let us be willing to go, to speak, to give, to pray. Let us be willing to be Your gentle hands in service to the lost. Praise the Lord of the harvest! Amen.

Jesus saw the huge crowd as he stepped from the boat, and he had compassion on them because they were like sheep without a shepherd. So he began teaching them many things.
MARK 6:34 NLT

STRENGTH IN GENTLENESS

*L*ord, I'm meditating on what it means to be gentle. Gentleness is one of the fruits of the Spirit, an attribute of Your character You long to see growing in us. It's mildness, calmness, quietness, placidness. It's restful, peaceful, tranquil. It's slow to react. It does not push itself forward. It is the opposite of harsh and rough.

It's a challenge to think of all those words as descriptors of Your character, Lord. You are strong, yet I have difficulty seeing the strength in gentleness. I tend to see it as weakness or passivity or lack of self-confidence. But how much more strength did it take to compassionately and patiently clothe the errant two in the garden and plan their future redemption than to annihilate them and start from scratch? How much more strength did it take to stay on that cross when You could have come down at any moment? How much more strength did it take to stand silent before Your accusers when You are the Word of Truth? How much more strength did it take to patiently explain the meaning of Your parables to a ragtag band of disciples than to march into Jerusalem at the head of a legion of angels and establish Your kingdom by force? Lord, let me follow You in gentleness and rest. Amen.

"Take my yoke upon you and learn from me, for I am gentle and humble in heart, and you will find rest for your souls."
MATTHEW 11:29 NIV

The Mother Load

*D*ear Lord, we pray today for the first, most basic, and most influential relationship. We pray for mothers. We pray for safety in childbirth, for patience with sleepless nights, for strength to meet endless needs. So much is expected of them today, and criticism—both from within and without—is rampant. The burden they feel—of never doing enough or *being* enough—is crushing.

We pray You will help struggling mothers see that they, as well as their precious children, are in Your hands. You gave them the children they have for Your own purposes, both to bless them and to grow them. They are right where they should be, and they are who You made them to be. They are enough. They are sufficient, because in You, they partake of Your divine sufficiency. Lord, give those worrying mothers Your peace. Give those endlessly striving mothers Your rest. Give those hovering, pushing mothers Your tenderness. And give them all Your wisdom to see that it's not their job—nor is it even within their capabilities—to save and sanctify another's soul. That is Your job, and we put our children in Your loving hands, knowing there is no safer place. Amen.

And they brought unto him also infants, that he would touch them. . . . But Jesus called them unto him, and said, Suffer little children to come unto me, and forbid them not; for of such is the kingdom of God.
Luke 18:15–16 kjv

The Gentle Gardener

I praise You, Lord, for the beauty of this morning. I praise You for the pale blue sky outside my window, washed with clouds. I praise You for the gentle breeze stirring the bare branches of the birch trees. I praise You for gray shadows on melting snow. I praise You for my quiet, warm house full of sleeping life. I praise You that even though we had a blizzard on the first day of spring, there is green life waiting under the snow. I praise You for the promise of daffodils and crocuses.

I repent, Lord, for my impatience and my lack of faith in Your promise that season will succeed season. I repent of my persistent lack of contentment, my wish to rush ahead of You. I repent of thinking where I am and who I am are not good enough. Thank You for here, for right now, for who I am, and for what is outside my window today. I know You are growing me, Lord, though it's often as invisible to me as the stirrings of a bulb under the snow. You have both uprooted me and allowed me to put down roots, and both have been for my good. I yield to Your seasons and Your timing, always perfect. Amen.

There is a time for everything, and a season for every activity under the heavens: a time to be born and a time to die, a time to plant and a time to uproot.
ECCLESIASTES 3:1–2 NIV

Flapping Tongues

$\mathcal{D}$ear Father, everywhere—in print, on television, on the internet—hyperbole seems to rule the day. The talking heads are loud and loquacious and loose with the truth. They seem to think the one with the best sound-bite wins. And so often that is the case. We don't take the time to listen to the quieter, less flashy voices that may have something different to say. We believe what everyone else believes.

Lord, the world is so complicated, and truth seems buried so far down under conflicting voices, facts, and experiences that it's difficult to reach and harder to recognize. We ask for Your wisdom. Help us separate fact from fiction and verity from mere verbiage. Forgive us for our contributions to the noise and confusion. Forgive us for thinking we must always add our two cents to any conversation. Forgive us for talking when we should be listening. Forgive us for letting the ridiculousness of this world provoke us into unkind or harsh speech. Since You are so near, Lord, our gentleness should be evident to everyone around us, but often it isn't. Give us wisdom, peace, and gentleness in the way we conduct ourselves and represent You in this loud world. Let our words be few and always cloaked with prayer. Amen.

Be not rash with your mouth, and let not your heart be hasty to utter a word before God. For God is in heaven, and you are on earth; therefore let your words be few.
ECCLESIASTES 5:2 AMPC

Telling the Old, Old Story

*D*ear Lord, every day I need to remind myself of the Gospel. I need to remember that I am a fallen creature in desperate need of a Savior. I need to remember the garden—both Eden and Gethsemane. I need to remember perfection and what we wanted instead. I need to remember that I both choose and am chosen. I need to remember that the work of salvation is finished on the cross and that no matter what good deeds I perform today, I was saved completely and finally on the day I first believed.

Thank You for the truth of God's holiness, man's rebellion, Jesus' sacrifice, and our response to this beautiful, messy story. Without the anchor of this old, old story—this truest, most precious story—I forget, and I drift. I drift into doubt, self-sufficiency, indifference, fear, and anxiety. The simple recital of the Gospel keeps me anchored in truth, right where I need to be. Prod me, Lord, through Your Spirit and the Spirit acting in my brothers and sisters in Christ, to tell myself this story daily. I want to write it on my heart. Every word. The sweetest story that ever was told. And let it be the tale I tell to those who don't know You. Amen.

Sing to the Lord, all the earth! Tell of his salvation from day to day. Declare his glory among the nations, his marvelous works among all the peoples!
1 Chronicles 16:23–24 esv

THE CHURCH IS GOD'S FAMILY

*D*ear Father, You tell us to make disciples of all people, baptizing them in the name of the Father, Son, and Holy Spirit and teaching them what it means to be part of Your family. We try to do this, Lord, but often we find ourselves pulling back from Your growing family. We are comfortable with the people we know, and all these new people change the dynamics of our safe little church world. They have needs, ideas, and desires that may pull us out of our comfort zones. They may challenge long-held beliefs. Their presence may change long-established relationships.

Lord, this thinking shows our sin. Forgive us for thinking of the church as "ours." It has only ever been Yours. It is created, sustained, and guided only by Your Spirit, and we are adopted into it through no merit of our own but only by Your grace. We tremble when we realize how we continually try to turn the church into a human institution. Pull us back from that, we pray. Remind us that the church is *Your* family and that we are all there—whether we have been part of a congregation for two decades or two weeks—by Your grace. We do not serve ourselves, but You—and one another. Amen.

And I also say to you that you are Peter, and on this rock I will build My church, and the gates of Hades shall not prevail against it.
MATTHEW 16:18 NKJV

The Balm of Gilead

$\mathcal{D}$ear Lord, we pray today for those who work to bring healing in war-torn places. We lift to You doctors, nurses, clinic staff, and aid workers of all kinds. Their jobs are often dangerous, and we ask You to protect them both physically and spiritually. Though they are surrounded by evil, Your Holy Spirit is the hedge of protection for their souls. Though they are exposed to disease and danger, You decide what can touch them and what cannot. Their jobs are difficult, and we ask that You give them strength to keep serving. Their jobs are often invisible, and we ask that You give them the contentment to keep working even without the world's accolades.

We know You said we will have trouble in this world. We know the poor will always be with us. We know nations will rise against nations. But that is just for now. Give us—and the people on the front lines—the firm conviction that, though the battle rages, victory is at hand. Give them a supernatural joy that is not an affront to suffering but a balm to soothe it. Thank You for the people who are Your hands and feet in places others dare not go. Amen.

How beautiful upon the mountains are the feet of him who brings good news, who proclaims peace, who brings glad tidings of good things, who proclaims salvation, who says to Zion, "Your God reigns!"
Isaiah 52:7 nkjv

ALL WILL BE HEALED

*D*ear Father in heaven, we are blessed to live in a time when diseases that once killed millions are now things of the past. We are blessed by the doctors and scientists who have innovatively perfected surgical techniques and developed antibiotics and x-rays. Thank You for the minds You have given humans that allow doctors today to heal people who would have died in past centuries. We recognize that their wisdom and creativity come ultimately from Your hand.

Forgive us for the pride that says we are in control of life and death. We may influence it, yes, but that is not the whole story. You allowed Job to be afflicted for Your purposes. You let a man be born blind to show Your glory. On earth, Jesus healed everyone He touched. Today He heals the soul of everyone who calls upon His name. If disease kills our bodies, we still will not die. The dead in Christ will rise! We will open our eyes in heaven and look down at our resurrected bodies. Paralyzed limbs will move. Crooked joints will be straightened. Diseased minds will be unclouded. Blind eyes will see. All will be healed—if not now, then in eternity. All praise to You for that sure hope. Amen.

And wherever he went—into villages, towns or countryside—they placed the sick in the marketplaces. They begged him to let them touch even the edge of his cloak, and all who touched it were healed.
MARK 6:56 NIV

CLING TO THE TRUTH

*L*ord, I praise You for being the Word made flesh, for always knowing exactly what to say, for being the voice that spoke creation into existence. All Your utterances are perfect. Your silence is perfect too.

Jesus spoke when it would have been easier to be silent and was silent when it would have been easier to speak. I repent, Lord, of my willful tongue and of the times I have spoken without thought. I repent of the more frequent times when I have deliberated and remained silent. I confess my fear. I'm afraid to speak because—especially in this digital age—words can never be *un-spoken.* I think and rethink how various people might react to my words. *Will they be angry? Will they think less of me? Will these words come back to haunt me?* I know You want us to be wise in the way we speak, but You also command us to fear You and not man. Let me not be like Pilate and equivocate with truth out of cowardice or indifference. He dared to stand before the true Light and say, "What is truth?" We ask for wisdom and boldness and for Your Spirit to speak through us, which is the only way we can navigate that narrow path. Amen.

"For this cause I was born, and for this cause I have come into the world, that I should bear witness to the truth. Everyone who is of the truth hears My voice."
JOHN 18:37 NKJV

Clay Vessels in His Hands

*D*ear Father, You are the potter; we are the clay. You are the maker; we are the *made*. We praise You for creating us just as we are. We praise You for how You continue to shape us. We praise You for having a purpose and a plan for both the strengths You have given us and our flaws. We are chipped but not crushed, cracked but not discarded, dented but still precious. You are gentle with our weaknesses, and Your strength becomes ours as You hold us in Your hands.

We don't have to hide our damaged parts, fearing we are no longer useful, that we're not beautiful, or that another hard knock will shatter us completely. We can live with hearts fully open to the world around us and eagerly looking forward to our inheritance. What freedom and peace in being created! What joy in being held! We do not have to—we cannot—do it on our own. We can't fit ourselves for Your kingdom; we can only be fitted for it. That is the gift of Your Spirit in us. We thank and praise You, the God who holds us in His mighty, glorious hands. Amen.

Strengthened with all might, according to his glorious power, unto all patience and longsuffering with joyfulness; giving thanks unto the Father, which hath made us meet to be partakers of the inheritance of the saints in light.
Colossians 1:11–12 KJV

Look Closer

Lord, I marvel at Your world. The closer I look, the more amazing I find it to be. Flower pollen, smudged on my nose, makes me sneeze and run to wipe it away. But under a microscope, I see each grain is a work of art, bizarre and intricate. A blizzard makes me sigh in anticipation of the shoveling ahead. But each snowflake is distinct from every other. How can that be?

Some things can't stand under scrutiny. But the closer I look into You, Lord, the more I am amazed. At every level, I see You are deeper, wider, stronger, more beautiful, and more loving than I could have imagined. You ask me to consider with awe and wonder the works of Your hands. But I rush about, busy as a bushel of ants, intent on my petty tasks. Forgive me. Remind me to stop and look and praise. I know of no surer way to find tranquility of soul than to engage in purposeful thanksgiving. I know of no better way to infuse my speech with gentleness than to remember how much I have been forgiven. To You be the glory in all things, large and small. Amen.

"I will consider all your works
and meditate on all your mighty deeds."
PSALM 77:12 NIV

Not Who I Once Was

*D*ear Lord, You are perfect and holy, a consuming fire. Your laws are perfect. Your ways are righteous. You are altogether different from me, though I am made in Your image. You are glorious. Your creation declares Your existence and Your power. There is none like You, and I praise You.

I am a tiny, imperfect voice singing Your praises. I, a muddy, filthy, wretched child, am riddled with sin. Today, Lord, I am chafing at the constraints of love. I don't want to give anything; I want to keep it all to myself. I want to do what *I* want to do. Forgive me. Thank You for showing me my sin, and for showing me Jesus, who did not refuse the requirements of love. Instead, because of His great love for us, He welcomed the nails that held Him to the cross. You, Lord, did not spare Your only Son, but You are so gentle with my sin. You could jerk me around as if I were a naughty child or shout at me with lightning. But You don't. You give me Your own Spirit to speak gently to my heart. Despite my sin, You are at work in me. I am not who I once was! Amen.

Who can discern their own errors? Forgive my hidden faults. . . . May these words of my mouth and the meditation of my heart be pleasing in your sight, LORD, my Rock and my Redeemer.
PSALM 19:12, 14 NIV

The Better Part

*D*ear Lord, we thank You for preserving in Your Word the stories of Your interactions with different kinds of people. Thank You for letting us hear how You talked to Adam and Eve, to Cain, to Abraham, to Moses, to Gideon, to the prophets. Thank You for preserving Jesus' conversations with the woman at the well, with Mary and Martha, with His disciples, with the Pharisees and scribes, with Nicodemus, with Pilate. Thank You for how much we learn about Your character when we study how You spoke to specific people.

I want to talk to others like Jesus did, with words full of grace, truth, and gentleness. Forgive me for how often I fall short. Forgive me for how often I become like Martha and grumble about everything to be done. Forgive me when, as she was, I'm worried and upset, and forgive me for how those self-imposed burdens poison my speech to those around me. Thank You for speaking to her as You did, so that, now, You can speak to me through those same words. Thank You that I can choose what Mary chose instead, and I praise You for the promise that it will not be taken away. Amen.

"Martha, Martha," the Lord answered, "you are worried and upset about many things, but few things are needed—or indeed only one. Mary has chosen what is better, and it will not be taken away from her."
Luke 10:41–42 niv

THE STRENGTH WE
HAVE IS ENOUGH

*L*ord, we thank You that You use weak, imperfect vessels. Moses stuttered. Timothy was young. Peter denied You. Paul had persecuted believers. Rahab was a prostitute. David was an adulterer and a murderer. Solomon worshipped false gods. Abraham was a liar.

We too are all these things and more; we have broken every commandment. But amazingly, You use us anyway. The beautiful, beautiful blood of Jesus washes all that away and covers us with His perfect, undefiled righteousness. We walk in that power! What can we do but praise You? We lift our hands to You, Lord—empty but filled with Your Spirit, broken but made new, weak but overflowing with strength from on high. Gideon thought there was no way he and his men could rescue Israel from the Midianites. And he was right. He couldn't do it. But You in Your sovereignty used the weakest army—three hundred men—to rout the enemy completely. The Midianites killed one another, and those who were not killed fled in terror. You told Gideon to advance with just the strength he had—no more— and You provided the victory. You don't ask us to be anything more than exactly who You made us to be. We rest and rejoice in that. Amen.

Then the LORD turned to him and said,
"Go with the strength you have, and rescue
Israel from the Midianites. I am sending you!"
JUDGES 6:14 NLT

Our Own Ears Will Hear Him

*L*ord, when my life is crazy, I remember how You brought order out of chaos. When I feel overwhelmed, I know You are the rock I can cling to. When my strength is gone, I discover You have strength to spare. When I don't know what to do, You whisper in my ear, "This is the way; walk in it." When I feel hopeless, I know Your kingdom is coming soon. When I'm scared, I know I rest in the shelter of Your wings. When worries overwhelm me, You tell me to be still and *know* You are God. When doubts and confusion assail me, You are the source of all wisdom and knowledge. When my tasks seem too great, I know Your yoke is easy and Your burden is light.

Thank You for these promises, Lord. I am clinging to them right now. I know I don't always trust Your promises; often I fret and cry and spin in discouraged circles before I remember that You are right there with me. I turn to worthless things for the peace and clarity I crave. Create in me, Lord, the habit of mind where I turn to You first in all circumstances—in sickness, in health, in plenty, in want, in praise. Amen.

> *Your own ears will hear him. Right behind*
> *you a voice will say, "This is the way you*
> *should go," whether to the right or to the left.*
> Isaiah 30:21 NLT

SECTION 9: *Self-Control*

REJECT OUR SIN

*J*esus, You are holy and perfectly righteous. Never, in all eternity, has any sin been found in You. You stood before Satan and were tempted beyond anything we can imagine. Have any of us ever gone without food for forty days or been offered the rule of the entire world or known that if we threw ourselves off a cliff, a legion of angels would bear us on their wings? You did not waver from the will of the Father. You lived the life that is now impossible for us, since Adam and Eve's fall in the long-ago garden and the inherited stain of sin that resulted.

We look at Your life, Lord, and we say we hate sin. We say it is against all You desire, and we condemn it in others. We say we want to stop sinning, but when the choice is before us, so often we continue holding and touching our sin. If we are completely honest, we must admit to admiring it. Lord, our sin is hideous, but we keep looking at it! It is ruinous, but we don't immediately reject it! Forgive us. And give us Your power to see our sin as You see it and to lay it down. Amen.

Be alert and of sober mind. Your enemy the devil prowls around like a roaring lion looking for someone to devour. Resist him, standing firm in the faith.
1 PETER 5:8–9 NIV

Pray Like a Child

*L*ord, we come here again, empty, with no burning desire for You in our hearts. Yet You ask us to come before You and present our requests. So as an act of obedience, we pray. As an act of obedience, we praise. Our small sacrifice—giving You back a few minutes of the life that was Your gift to us in the first place—is nothing, but You count it as worship. You are a God who knows us to be worse than we can imagine, yet You treat us as more righteous than we can ever be.

Thank You, Lord. We confess that our minds wander; draw us back, again and again, into Your presence. We confess that we doubt You are listening; remind us that You are near. We confess that we doubt Your power; show it to us, Lord. We confess that we don't understand how prayer works; give us the discipline to turn to You anyway, until praying becomes as natural as breathing. We cannot demand, yet You tell us to ask. We cannot control Your timing, but You tell us to *keep* asking. We cannot understand this, so we ask You to increase our faith until it is as unshakable as a child's. Amen.

Listen to my cry for help, my King and my God,
for I pray to no one but you. Listen to my voice in
the morning, LORD. Each morning I bring my
requests to you and wait expectantly.
PSALM 5:2–3 NLT

No Fear of Man

$\mathcal{L}$ord, frightening people are abroad in the world today. Terrorists. Con artists. Identity thieves. Scammers. Tyrants with power over a nation and tyrants with power over just a few. People who delight in spreading rumors and dissent. Fearmongers. Warmongers. Alarmists. We have always been evil, but our ability to destroy has increased exponentially. We could destroy the world, and we probably will if You give us enough time.

Forgive us for our selfishness and shortsightedness. Forgive us for the sin that so easily entangles us and trips us. We do what is easy and comfortable most of the time, not what pleases You or is best for Your creation and the people around us. Give us the self-control to make wise, godly choices in these unwise, ungodly days. We *will* look different from our neighbors. We *will* look different from some of our family members. That is one of Your promises! Help us not to fear what will happen when others see that difference. Help us welcome it as the mark of being in Your service. Help us not to fear others—whether close by or across the globe—but to fear only You. A right, reverent fear of You is where all wisdom begins. In praise and thanksgiving and trust, amen.

> *The LORD is my light and my salvation;*
> *whom shall I fear? the LORD is the strength*
> *of my life; of whom shall I be afraid?*
> PSALM 27:1 KJV

SERVING WHERE I STAND

*D*ear Father, every good and perfect gift is from You, and I thank You. I thank You for my friends, my health, my house, my talents, my blessings, my church, my town. I don't pause enough to thank You for all those gifts. Often, I think of them as burdens, and I think of my responsibilities as a type of slavery. Forgive me. Help me recognize where the true slavery lies: those idols of comfort and ease I've fashioned for myself through daydreams and despair. Free me from that, Lord, so I can worship You in spirit and in truth.

Thank You for the freedom—when I recognize it—in serving right where I stand, even if where I am sometimes seems like a dry and barren wilderness. I can look behind me to the imagined perfection of the past, and I can look ahead to what I desire but You have not given. Or I can choose to look at the only two places that are *real*: right here, where I'm standing at this moment, and at You. Purify my heart for worship, Lord. Amen.

Therefore I. . .beg you to lead a life worthy
of your calling, for you have been called by God.
EPHESIANS 4:1 NLT

A Closer Walk

*D*ear Father, again I'm meditating on desire and how its claws grip me past all reason. I'm like a little child who wants his one marshmallow, even though he is promised two if he can wait just a little longer. I want, I want, I want. Now. Now. Now. Like Eve in the garden, gazing on that glistening fruit, I take what looks good in the moment, despite how it might harm me or damage my relationship with You and others. I want to say no to the sins of anger, gluttony, gossip, and greed that beset me, but they feel so good—even though I already know I will regret them—so I vent, I eat, I speak, I buy, I take.

Instead of trusting that You have given me, as You promise, everything I need for life and godliness, I try to create contentment on my own terms. I try to draw closer to You through false emotionalism instead of through simple acts of obedience. And every time, these things fail to satisfy. I am left wanting, and my spiritual muscles are weaker. All this is to say, I'm sorry. Lead me in the baby steps that will bring me eventually to a closer walk with You. Amen.

Create in me a clean heart, O God, and renew a right,
persevering, and steadfast spirit within me.
Cast me not away from Your presence and
take not Your Holy Spirit from me.
Psalm 51:10–11 AMPC

About Planks and Specks

$\mathcal{D}$ear Lord, we are so often blind to our own sin and blinded by it. We can't see it, and we can't even see the way it compromises our vision. Even David—who is called a man after God's own heart—dug himself deeper and deeper in sin, blind to its hideousness, until Nathan pointed at him and said, "You are the man!"

We praise You for Nathan and others like him who are willing to speak the truth. Surround us with truth tellers, Lord. We praise You also for the Spirit that lives in us that can awaken us to our sin before it's too late. Unrepentant sin leads to death; Your Word is clear about that. We say we don't want that, yet every day we make choices that lead us in that direction. We rail at the sin in the world, yet we ignore the sin in our own hearts. We pray that the Spirit will sharpen our senses to our own sin, that we will feel the specks that pain us and cloud our sight, and that we will welcome the washing of water through Your Spirit, the Word of truth, and the Spirit speaking through other believers. Amen.

Husbands, love your wives, even as Christ also loved the church, and gave himself for it; that he might sanctify and cleanse it with the washing of water by the word, that he might present it to himself a glorious church.
EPHESIANS 5:25–27 KJV

Teach Us

*D*ear Father, You are so willing for us to grow in wisdom and knowledge. Thank You for all the teachers who have had a part in my growth. Thank You for my Sunday school teachers, elementary and high school teachers, camp counselors, professors, and pastors. Thank You for the family members and friends You gave me who taught me so much. Thank You for the authors and speakers from whom I have had the privilege of learning. Thank You for my parents, my first teachers. Thank You for Your Holy Spirit, my constant guide.

I confess the times I have been hardhearted and rejected the advice of my wise teachers. Forgive me. I pray that I will grow to be more open and moldable and humble, not stubborn like Pharaoh. He crashed headlong into the high walls of God's mighty power over and over but would not desist or repent. Let me be willing to learn from the wisdom and experience of others, instead of having to learn every lesson through the crucible of life. Thank You also for the blessing of Your Word; by it is Your servant warned. Lord, soften my heart so I can learn from You. Amen.

[The decrees of the Lord] are more precious than gold, than much pure gold; they are sweeter than honey, than honey from the honeycomb. By them is your servant warned; in keeping them there is great reward.
PSALM 19:10–11 NIV

For Our Leaders

*L*ord, we pray today for the self-control of people in high positions. We pray they will act with wisdom and justice, not self-interest. We pray they will avoid the snares of graft, cronyism, and partisanship. We pray for their strength against temptations we can only imagine. We pray for their safety from people who wish them harm. We pray that if they do not know You, You will bring people to them who can be a force for godliness and repentance. We pray for their wisdom in making difficult decisions that can never seem to please everyone. All true strength and wisdom come from You, and we ask that You bestow it on the people who make decisions for the many.

We need You, Lord, in those inner circles and high places, which so easily become temples of ungodliness. Thank You for reminding us to pray for our leaders. Bring their names continually before us for intercession. Thank You for putting them into position. We don't always understand why we have the leaders we do. We think, *Surely someone else would be better*, yet Your Word is clear in Romans 13: You have established every authority. But we can always pray. Help us to do so, fervently and continually. Amen.

Be wise now therefore, O ye kings: be instructed,
ye judges of the earth. Serve the LORD with fear,
and rejoice with trembling.
PSALM 2:10–11 KJV

WAYWARD THOUGHTS

*D*ear Lord, though we inhabit these miraculous bodies You gave us—for which we thank You—we are often mystified by the thoughts that enter and depart our minds. From where do they come? To where do they fly? We are creatures with both body and spirit, but we don't quite understand that unique intersection. We often feel at the mercy of our thoughts, but we long to have our minds controlled by the Spirit.

We need Your power to redirect our wayward thoughts, over and over. If we feel abandoned, remind us of Gethsemane. If we feel hopeless, remind us of the joy set before us in heaven. If we feel anxious about finances, remind us that we are co-heirs with Christ and have an eternal, incorruptible inheritance. If we feel defeated by our sin, remind us of Your triumph at the cross. If we feel afraid, remind us that You have already won the victory. As Paul says, it is better by far to depart this life and be with Christ, but You hold our days in Your hands. And we are here now. Help us to number our days aright, not to waste them in idle, fruitless thinking. Remind us to apply Your criteria to our thoughts: Is it true? Is it right? Is it lovely? Is it admirable? Help us think about such things. Amen.

So teach us to number our days, that we
may present to You a heart of wisdom.
PSALM 90:12 NASB

Exodus Story

*L*ord, I began to consider the claims of Jesus because someone told me how He was real in her life. She spoke of Him as her friend, and He was clearly not the man I thought He was. Over time, the small seed planted in my heart grew and flourished. Thank You for her faithful testimony, which led to my salvation.

All through the Old Testament, You remind Your people to tell of Your mighty acts, Your judgments, Your mercy, Your faithfulness. We are to tell of them when we sit at home and when we walk along the road, when we lie down and when we get up. We are to talk about them in the great assembly, in the quiet of our homes, to our children, to foreigners in our land. And, Lord, the drawing power of Your Holy Spirit through the testimonies of believers is such that it frequently leads to salvation for others. I praise You for how Your power was made real in my life. I praise You for how it has been real in the lives of so many other believers. Because of You, our stories are powerful. Remind me to tell my exodus story: how I was rescued from slavery and brought into new life. Amen.

"Praise the Lord," Jethro said, "for he has rescued you from the Egyptians and from Pharaoh. . . .
I know now that the Lord is greater than all other gods, because he rescued his people."
Exodus 18:10–11 nlt

CHANGING THE WORLD
WITH PRAYER

*D*ear Lord, I can control some things and some I cannot. The older I get, the larger the second category becomes, the more I recognize how little control I have. I can control when I get into bed, but You still my heart and mind into sleep. I can brush and primp and powder, but You have given me my gray hairs and crow's-feet. I can drive as carefully and as mindfully as possible, but You control whether I arrive safely at my destination. I can, with the help of Your Spirit and Your precious Word, live a godly life, but You determine my end and beginning.

I do praise and thank You for the way Your hand has guided my life and a whole host of things that are far beyond my control: most other people, world events, geological disasters, war and peace. Yet even as I pray, You remind me that prayer is a lever that can lift the most impossible stone. I can move even mountains, if it's Your will. Thank You, Lord, for that reminder. Remind me to pray for that which seems the most improbable, the most hopeless, the most tangled. You are the God of just such things. In praise and awe, amen.

Jesus replied, "Truly I tell you, if you have faith and
do not doubt. . .you can say to this mountain, 'Go,
throw yourself into the sea,' and it will be done."
MATTHEW 21:21 NIV

It Is Enough

*L*ord, again, I turn to You in repentance. I didn't get what I wanted; what I saw as my right (to get a good night's rest) was infringed upon. My anger, hot and ugly, boiled up in an instant against one of Your precious people. A little person, Lord, who couldn't sleep and couldn't tell me what was wrong. And instead of offering love and comfort in Your strength—because that's all I have and *it is enough*—I offered impatience and hard words.

Forgive me. I have prayed this same prayer so many times, and I praise You that Your mercy toward me is never exhausted. I ask that You blot out the memory of my anger in the heart of my little one. And I turn my situation to praise, because that is the only thing to do with it. I praise You for that long night. I praise You for the child who cried for comfort. I praise You for where I am when I'm at the end of my own strength. I praise You that Your mercies are new every morning. I praise You for how You understand my wordless cries perfectly. I praise You that You can use everything for Your glory. Amen.

Follow God's example, therefore, as dearly loved children and walk in the way of love, just as Christ loved us and gave himself up for us as a fragrant offering and sacrifice to God.
Ephesians 5:1–2 niv

Pray at All Times

$\mathcal{D}$ear Lord, You ask us to come before Your throne in prayer at all times and on every occasion. You don't specify when we should pray or what position our body should be in. We come to You on Your own terms, yes, with proper reverence and awe, but we no longer approach Your throne with dread. Unlike Esther, we do not come before the King in peril of our lives. We thank You that we can approach Your throne with confidence. Because of Jesus, ceremony is finished.

We are the temple of the Holy Spirit now, and with the covering of Jesus' blood, we are as perfect, righteous, and beautiful in Your sight as the embroidered linen curtains, golden lampstands, and bronze altar of Your original tabernacle. Now we are the aroma of Christ, sweeter than any incense. Because of Jesus, You see us this way, no longer sin-scarred and broken, but beautiful. Remind us through Your Spirit to pray, to talk to You, the God of the universe who loves us so much that He sent Jesus to die for us. If You love us that much, why are we not continually talking to You as we sit, stand, and walk? If You love us that much, why are we content to hold You at arm's length? Draw us in, Lord, to Your precious, bleeding side. Amen.

Pray in the Spirit at all times and on every occasion.
Stay alert and be persistent in your prayers
for all believers everywhere.
Ephesians 6:18 nlt

Garden

*F*ather, I am continually surprised by how hard this life is. I don't know why that should be so—why I should always be expecting it to be different—unless I was created for something else. Does a fish ever long for dry land? Does a falcon long for solid ground under its feet? This is what I long for, Lord: safety, peace, contentment, rest, true communion with You and others, springtime, satisfying and productive work, flowers.

Adam and Eve had that for a little while in the garden of Eden, and I thank You for giving us a picture of what You had in mind for us in the beginning. But their legacy to us is a very different world, scarred by flood, famine, disaster, war, and greed. This is no garden, Lord. That anything grows at all is a miracle and a gift. But thank You that I feel like a nomad and a stranger here. That too is a gift from You. Thank You for the longings in my heart that point me to my true home, which is to come and is prepared for me. And I thank You that when You look at me through the covering of Jesus' blood, You can still say, "It is very good." Amen.

God saw all that he had made, and it was very good.
And there was evening, and there was morning—
the sixth day. Thus the heavens and the earth
were completed in all their vast array.
GENESIS 1:31–2:1 NIV

No Reason to Boast

$\mathcal{L}$ord, just when I think I'm making some progress toward godliness, when my anger and my tongue are under control and my good deeds seem to outweigh my sins, I fall again—spectacularly. All my illusions crumble, and I see myself as You do: a sinner in desperate need of a Savior. Thank You for showing me my need in such painful ways. Thank You for constraining me with my own sin, lest I wander far from Your side. I don't want to boast in my sin, but it does serve a purpose in my life. It reminds me daily of my position in relation to You: both perfectly righteous *and* utterly dependent on the blood of Jesus.

I am so easily fooled into self-sufficiency. Forgive me for thinking I can do anything without You. I need You every hour. You chose me, Lord; I did nothing to deserve salvation. I repent of my sin today. I repent of my good deeds too. They are not *mine* but Yours. I ask that You give me the self-control not to clutch those fine deeds tightly. They are gifts from You too, so I have no reason to boast in them. In thanksgiving and praise, amen.

So now there is no condemnation for those who belong
to Christ Jesus. And because you belong to him,
the power of the life-giving Spirit has freed you
from the power of sin that leads to death.
Romans 8:1–2 nlt

"I Don't Know"

*D*ear Lord, You know the answer to every question ever asked. You know the answers to all our unspoken, half-formulated questions, and You know the answers to the questions we've not yet stumbled upon. You are wisdom. You are the Word. You are eternal. You, Yourself, *are* the answer.

I struggle to understand little parts of You and Your world, and I stand in awe and wonder and praise at the magnificence of Your mind. Thank You, Lord, for who You are and for creating in me the capacity to wonder. Let me rest there, in childlike awe. But also give me the self-discipline to do the hard work—to learn who You are, why I believe, what I believe, and why what I believe is true so I have answers ready when You prompt me to speak to others. I also ask for the self-control and wisdom not to be a chatterbox who must have an answer for every question, who thinks she must fill every silence with words. You are larger than all my words. Let me be willing to say, "I don't know." Let Your Spirit work through my words, as well as in the silent places where I have no more words. Amen.

Walk in wisdom toward those who are outside,
redeeming the time. Let your speech always be
with grace, seasoned with salt, that you may
know how you ought to answer each one.
Colossians 4:5–6 nkjv

WHEN WE WAKE

*D*ear Lord, we sometimes wonder what waking up in heaven will be like. Will it be like going to sleep with a bad case of the flu and waking up completely well? Like falling asleep in the middle of a winter's blizzard and waking to sunshine and spring? Getting into bed with bombs rattling the casements and screams in the streets, and then being wakened by singing? Going to sleep destitute and hungry and waking with the fulfillment of every desire standing before us in the flesh?

It will be all that and more, Lord, and we thank You for that hope, secured with a promise. So often, though, we *do* go to sleep with worries, grief, anger, or anxiety pressing on us. We live here, and it is often hard. Comfort us. Be with us. Help us live well and at the same time wait breathlessly for the eternal Son to rise. We can't do that on our own. Without Your Spirit we can't live in that tension; we teeter back and forth between rejecting the blessings of this life and thinking they are all we have. But hope flows backward and forward between earth and heaven because You, God, became a man. Praise be to our living Lord. Amen.

And we desire each one of you to show the same
earnestness to have the full assurance of hope until
the end. . .imitators of those who through faith
and patience inherit the promises.
HEBREWS 6:11–12 ESV

SECTION 10: *Grace*

GRACE IS GREATER

*L*ord, Your law is hard yet beautiful, a picture of what we lost and what we will someday gain. It is a picture of how we were created to function both in relationship with God and with other people. But the purpose of the law is not to restrain our behavior, though it sometimes does. Its purpose is to drive us to Jesus and keep us there. Its purpose is to show us our need for a Savior. It reminds us that we cannot save ourselves.

Lord, we cannot imagine living in a world with no murder, no theft, and no adultery. We cannot imagine what the world would look like if nobody wanted what other people have, if nobody ever placed anything on the altar of their heart except You. But we praise You because that is exactly what You had in mind, and Your purposes from the beginning cannot be thwarted. Grace has won. Perfection is coming. One day we will no longer struggle with sin. And we praise You in the meantime for the grace in which we walk, forgiven and set free, from what *was* to what *will be*. Amen.

Your word is a lamp to my feet and a light to my path.
I have sworn an oath and confirmed it, to keep your
righteous rules. I am severely afflicted; give me life,
O Lord, according to your word!
PSALM 119:105–107 ESV

To Serve as We Have Been Served

*L*ord, so many religions put the deeds of their followers on a scale—good deeds on one side, bad deeds on the other. They hope—but can never be sure—their good deeds will outweigh the bad and earn them admittance into paradise. We praise You that You are holy and just and that our sins do require an accounting. And we praise You for the perfect sacrifice of Your Son, who paid the sin-debt that would have condemned us to hell. We can never swing the balance in our own favor; we are forever bankrupted by our sin.

But the grace extended to us on the cross does not number our sins. Instead, that grace washes them all away. Our debt is canceled, the scales forever tipped in our favor. And that is the same grace we can extend to those around us. We pray, Lord, that we will not tally our service and sacrifices to others and weigh them against what we are given in return. Help us to forgive the same offense seventy times seven. You gave everything; let us be willing to do the same. Help us to give and give, without counting the cost, just as Jesus did. In His strength, amen.

"Give, and it will be given to you. A good measure, pressed down, shaken together and running over, will be poured into your lap. For with the measure you use, it will be measured to you."
Luke 6:38 niv

Grace Floats

*D*ear Lord, when sadness and depression come creeping like a fog, they cloud my sight. Often nothing radical has changed in my life, but I *see* differently. Normal hardships become magnified into tragedies. Relationship difficulties seem insurmountable. Nothing seems certain except disaster. All my blessings sink into a sea of hopelessness.

I ask for both forgiveness and help. Forgive me for the sin of despair. Forgive me for forgetting You. Why do I forget You love me? Why do I forget You created the universe and everything in it? Why do I forget You are all-powerful? When the creature tries to become the creator, despair is the natural result. Reorder my thinking, Lord. In these times, I also ask You to send the Comforter, Your Holy Spirit, to me. I need Him to remind me—continually and firmly—what grace really is: God's riches at Christ's expense. Remind me of the riches, remind me of Christ, remind me of the cost. Remind me that grace is where I'm standing *now*, even when it doesn't feel like it, even when I feel as though I'm sinking, because grace floats. And gracious Lord, I will sing praises to You. Praise is transformative. You are transformative. Do Your work in me. Amen.

Therefore, since we have been justified through faith, we have peace with God through our Lord Jesus Christ, through whom we have gained access by faith into this grace in which we now stand.
Romans 5:1–2 niv

Name Them

*L*ord, as I took a walk yesterday, You brought to mind an old song: "Count your blessings, name them one by one." For the first time, I heard those words in a different light. *Name them*, I thought. *Your blessings have names: they are people!* Now, I know I am no pauper, and Your many blessings to me have included material blessings such as houses, jobs, money, cars, and clothes. But Your blessings are primarily people. When I think of Your riches given to me at Christ's expense, I remember other believers, also saved by grace.

Thank You for those people. Thank You for my spouse, children, friends, and family. Thank You for my pastor, the leaders of my church, and the people who serve as everything from Sunday school teachers to greeters to sidewalk shovelers. Thank You for those who visit the lonely and make meals for the sick. Thank You for those who serve, unknown. Thank You for the believers in my life who have reminded me of Your goodness and faithfulness when I needed it most. Thank You for those who shared truth with me when I was still in darkness. Thank You for Paul, who continually thanked You for the people he ministered to and with: Timothy, Silvanus, Stephanas, Fortunatus, Achaicus, Tychicus, Philemon, Apphia, and Archippus. Thank You for Your people; You know their names. Amen.

We give thanks to God always for all of you,
constantly mentioning you in our prayers.
1 Thessalonians 1:2 esv

BLIND SPOTS

*D*ear Lord, some things about me seem to rub against others and cause friction. I have ways of expressing myself and habits of mind and body I think are just personality quirks, but they may not be; they may be sin. I am easy on myself, Lord. I treat myself as a beloved pet who's allowed to make messes in the house and bark at strangers just because she is cute and soft.

Forgive me, God. I am no pet. I am a child of the King, co-heir with Your Son, Jesus, and I am being sanctified for Your use and glory in this present age and in the kingdom to come. It is both humbling and exhilarating that I could be useful to You. That You would care so much about me that You would take the time to sanctify me. The paradox is—showing Your love for me even more—that You don't need me. I am weak and small and powerless, and anything I do can be magnified into usefulness only by the power of the Holy Spirit working in me. I pray that Your Holy Spirit and other believers will speak into my life with grace and truth and show me where I'm weak so I can become strong and useful to You. Amen.

> *"And I will ask the Father, and he will give you*
> *another Advocate, who will never leave you.*
> *He is the Holy Spirit, who leads into all truth."*
> JOHN 14:16–17 NLT

Come as We Are

*D*ear Lord, we praise You that no sin is so terrible that it cannot be covered with the atoning blood of Jesus Christ, that no place is so far away from You that we cannot be brought back by the power of His perfect sacrifice. You ask us to come as we are, and we don't need to clean up our act first—because we can't. We come before You stained with the sins of years and generations: rebellion, anger, greed, lust, idolatry, adultery, murder, gossip, dissension, cruelty, selfishness. We are broken and helpless before the law.

But Jesus is the law's fulfillment: He is the perfect law that brings freedom. Lord, we recognize our bondage to sin today, both the sins we committed and the sins we wanted to commit but didn't out of cowardice. We recognize no one is righteous, not one, and only by Your grace and providence are we not terrorists, mass murderers, and tyrants. We praise You for sending Your Son into this world. We praise You for His perfect sacrifice on our behalf. We praise You for revealing Your truth to us through other believers, the Bible, and the Holy Spirit. We praise You for the grace that is greater than all our sin. We praise You! Amen.

For Christ has already accomplished the purpose
for which the law was given. As a result,
all who believe in him are made right with God.
Romans 10:4 nlt

Sailing

*L*ord, I bounce between self-sufficiency and despair with the same seasick instability James's double-minded man had. When life is going well, I forget You and think I'm doing it all on my own—and quite well, thank you. When life is hard, when difficulties and sins mount up and block the sunlight, I can just as easily forget You. I think where I am at that moment is where I will always be, and in that darkness, I forget the Light is coming.

Forgive me, Lord. Help me fix my eyes on You in every situation. Free me from the self-sufficiency that is the opposite of depending on grace. Any strength I think I possess—health, wealth, success, good relationships—is fodder for pride. Free me also from the blindness of despair, which is also a type of self-sufficiency, looking only at myself. The walls of my own mind become the limits of my future. You are outside of all that; You are larger than what I take pride in and what blinds me. Help me rest and remain in the grace-full space between those extremes. You give the strength that allows me to succeed today and the hope that lets me look forward to tomorrow. Trials come in many guises, Lord, and only Your Spirit can guide our frail ships. Amen.

*Consider it pure joy, my brothers and sisters, whenever
you face trials of many kinds, because you know that
the testing of your faith produces perseverance.*
James 1:2–3 niv

Living in Us

*D*ear Father, Adam and Eve walked with You in the garden of Eden in the cool of the day. Sometimes we're jealous of that closeness. We long to walk with You too. But what was lost has been redeemed with something greater, and we repent of our sinful nostalgia.

We don't have You walking beside us in the physical sense Adam and Eve did; nor can we see Jesus' face and dusty feet next to us on the road the way the disciples did as they walked from Bethany to Jerusalem. But again, Lord, we praise You for doing an even greater work through the redemption offered by Your Son. Now You live in us. You can speak to our hearts wherever we are. Now we have Your very Word. We can carry it in our pockets. We can read it wherever we go, and if we memorize it, we can never lose it. Help us to live not with a misplaced longing for what is past, but with an attitude of continual praise and celebration for what has been given us. You are living in us now, Lord. Give us ears to hear Your Spirit speak. In praise and expectation, we lift Your name. Amen.

Everything that the Father has is Mine. That is what I meant when I said that He [the Spirit] will take the things that are Mine and will reveal (declare, disclose, transmit) it to you.
JOHN 16:15 AMPC

THE COMFORTER

*L*ord Jesus, before You died, You promised Your disciples You would send them a Comforter to guide them into all truth. Your Spirit came with wind, fire, and transformation. God in us—how we marvel, just as Mary did. Your Spirit is a comforter, and we praise You for that. Your Spirit also convicts of sin, and we thank You for that too because often it's not comfort we need but a stern reminder that in this world we will have trouble. We *can* take comfort in that because of the unalterable fact that You have overcome the world.

That truth is written in past tense. It's not happening now, and it's not going to happen sometime; it has already taken place. By dying on the cross and being raised again, You conquered sin and death, once and for all. Sanctification is the process by which we too can live as overcomers without everything "fixed." Let us not be drinkers of milk but partakers of Your flesh. Let us not look for easy roads, but be willing to walk high, stony hills—as You did—and tread narrow paths. Let us not hide but be willing to stand up, naked, before mockers. Comforted through all this, we become like You, Jesus. Amen.

"My soul magnifies the Lord, and my spirit rejoices in God my Savior, for he has looked on the humble estate of his servant. For behold, from now on all generations will call me blessed."

LUKE 1:46–48 ESV

GRACE-FORGED ARMOR

*L*ord, You have given me so much: all Your riches now and to come. I am blessed beyond measure, and I thank You for giving me a moment's peace and quiet to contemplate that. Is this a shallow faith? I don't think so, because it has been tested through years and tears. Is this an unreasonable hope? No. You have proved true in other ways in the past, so I believe You will be proved faithful to the promise of eternal life also.

I think the question is whether I'm depending on anything but grace. Is the blood of Jesus Christ, shed on the cross for the payment of my sins, really my only hope in this life and the next? I pray, Lord, that You will show me the hard, shiny places in my life that are impervious to grace. Pry them off, wash me clean, and clothe me with the armor of Your making, not my own. I ask that You allow those naked places to be a witness to others about the power of Your love. Give me the courage to speak of my pride and sin and redemption. Let me, in some small way, be an encourager to others, showing them You are sufficient. In praise and thanksgiving, amen.

Finally, be strong in the Lord and in the strength of his might. Put on the whole armor of God, that you may be able to stand against the schemes of the devil.
EPHESIANS 6:10–11 ESV

YOKES

*F*ather, if Your yoke is easy and Your burden is light, why do I feel so tired? If I feel oppressed by everything I must do and all the demands being placed upon me, am I really wearing *Your* yoke? Perhaps I have allowed myself to be strapped into a yoke not of Your making. Because it doesn't feel easy or light. Instead of counting my blessings, I counted all the tasks I had to do. Instead of counting it all joy, I allowed my heart to soak in bitterness and become sour. Instead of working while it was day, I became overwhelmed—and did nothing.

Forgive me for placing productivity on the altar of my heart. Forgive me for my anger with the people who slowed me down. Help me find a peace and balance that will please You and give me the space and silence to hear You speak. An amazing promise is in these verses: when You restore my joy, when You create in me a willing spirit, sinners will turn back to You. Joy and perseverance bring salvation to others. What a promise! What joy to have a part in that! In faith and hope, amen.

Restore to me the joy of your salvation and grant me a willing spirit, to sustain me. Then I will teach transgressors your ways, and sinners will turn back to you.
PSALM 51:12–13 NIV

THE COMPARISON TRAP

*D*ear Father, Your world is full of people, and each one is unique. We have similarities—being made in Your likeness—but since You first said, "Let us make man in our image," no two people on earth have been the same. So often, we look at others in envy; they have some talent, personality trait, or attribute we lack and wish we had. We feel imperfect and lesser in comparison. Forgive us for our discontent. Can the clay tell the potter how it should be formed? Who are we to complain about how You made us? Can we understand the mind of God?

You have had Your purposes in mind from the very beginning, and You have allowed us—such as we are—to be a part of that plan. We thank You for Your infinite creativity. Thank You for making us who we are. Thank You for the gifts You have given us, and thank You for the gifts You have given to others. Give us rest from the discontent that plagues us. Let us instead be thankful and satisfied with ourselves—not with our sin, of course, but as vessels formed for Your use and glory. In You, we are enough. Amen.

This is what the LORD says. . . "Do you question what
I do for my children? Do you give me orders about
the work of my hands? I am the one who made
the earth and created people to live on it."
ISAIAH 45:11–12 NLT

RIPPLES

*D*ear Lord, Your Word is amazing. It is the richest of foods and never grows stale. It speaks to all people in all times and places. It's made of numerous parts written by diverse authors, yet it tells one continuous, cohesive story. It is unchanged over thousands of years. It is marks on a page *and* the voice of God that answers the sin, death, and despair in the world.

You say Your Word will not return void, meaning when it is read and spoken, those words reverberate and travel like the ripples from a stone thrown in still water. But unlike those concentric ripples, the waves from Your Word never dissipate. That is the mystery and majesty of how You operate. We can't see much of the Spirit's working, but it is there, and more real and effective than anything we can touch. Just as we see only a tiny fraction of all the light waves that exist—just red, yellow, green, blue, indigo, and violet—Your Word is working in ways beyond our perception. We praise You for that power. Give us faith to speak Your Word to others, knowing that despite what we may see, You are working in and through it. Amen.

So shall my word be that goes out from my mouth; it shall not return to me empty, but it shall accomplish that which I purpose, and shall succeed in the thing for which I sent it.
ISAIAH 55:11 ESV

Questions and Answers

*L*ord, I have so many questions about how to live in a way that pleases You. It seems impossible sometimes. I see hatred all around me. *Can I love?* I see injustice. *Can I treat others fairly?* I see sickness. *Can I bring healing and comfort?* I see broken relationships. *Can I show what peace and reconciliation look like?* I see fear. *Can I offer assurance and hope?* I see anger. *Can I be kind?* I see all these sins around me, yet I know they are in me too. Only through the Spirit working in and through me can I become part of the solution, not part of the problem.

Lord, You are the only remedy for this hurting world. You bring peace, healing, comfort, reconciliation, assurance, and hope. Your kindness is unfailing and everlasting. I pray that Your Spirit will fill me and spill out so I can answer yes to all those hard questions. On my own, it's impossible. Even when I want to say yes, I so often say no by my actions. Teach me to cry out to You, knowing that You are listening to me and acting for me and loving me, even when You seem silent. I am crying out now, Lord. Amen.

I call out to you; save me and I will keep your statutes. I rise before dawn and cry for help; I have put my hope in your word.
Psalm 119:146–147 niv

LIVING IN THE WATERS

*D*ear Father, the day of Your Son's return may be tomorrow, or it may be long years past our death. Only You know; not even the Son knows the hour and the day. So until then, we persevere in obedience, walking upstream against the current of this world. Give us grace and strength to enjoy the feeling of rocks under our feet, the push of water against our legs. Sometimes we fret and sigh as we go through trials, seeing others, as it were, floating downstream on inner tubes, laughing and splashing. But we know what lies downstream of holiness, Lord, so we press on toward You.

Help us cry out as we go—about the beauty of the upstream way and where we are headed. Help us turn people around midstream. Lord, You are the living water; You are the water that gives us life. Flow in, through, and around us. Draw us to the Fount of all blessing, from which everything good flows. We love You and praise You for the hope You have poured into us, without stint, without cost. The closer we get to You, the more pure and delicious the water becomes. That is hope. In praise and longing, amen.

On that day living waters shall flow out from Jerusalem. . . .
And the LORD will be king over all the earth. On that
day the LORD will be one and his name one.
ZECHARIAH 14:8–9 ESV

WORSHIP

*D*ear Lord, we long to cultivate Your fruit in our lives, but we can do so only by fixing our eyes on the source of that goodness, that faithfulness, that joy in worship. Teach us to worship You in spirit and truth. Let us not be fooled into thinking we are worshipping You with cheap emotionalism. Let us be wary of preaching to one another when we should be falling on our knees in adoration. Guard our minds from false doctrine in worship: words with rhyme but no truth. To come into the presence of the living God is a fearful thing, but that is what You ask us to do in worship. Are we crying, "Holy, holy, holy is the Lord God Almighty, who was and is and is to come"?

We ask, with trembling, that You purify our worship. We ask that You burn away anything not of You. We acknowledge how scary it is to stand, naked, before Your throne in worship, and we repent of what we use—even in church—to shield ourselves from Your beauty and holiness. We can't do this right, Lord, so we yield to Your Spirit, who promises to guide us into the truth. Help us to listen—and obey. Amen.

But the hour cometh, and now is, when the true worshippers shall worship the Father in spirit and in truth: for the Father seeketh such to worship him.

JOHN 4:23 KJV

Praying for the Impossible

The disasters we see around us, Lord, are too great for us. Even the calamities within our own relationships are more than we can manage. And our own hearts are minefields of sin and trouble. You ask us to pray—and say we will be able to move mountains—but so often we don't even try. We long to be bold and persistent in prayer, but the reality is most of the time we're content with our troubles. They are familiar, and, if not comfortable, at least more comfortable than Your awesome power.

Forgive us for our lack of faith, our fear, and our little love. We cast all these burdens at Your feet. We cannot carry them, but You can. You can move mountains, and You have. You made a way where there was no way by redeeming fallen mankind at the cross. You picked us up and carried us—with all our sin and pride and foolishness—and are carrying us still. Nothing is too heavy for our Savior to bear; nothing exists that You cannot make new. And so, with fear and trembling, we pray for the impossible: for Your kingdom to come and Your will be done, both in us and in the world. Amen.

And as he was praying, heaven was opened and the Holy Spirit descended on him in bodily form like a dove. And a voice came from heaven: "You are my Son, whom I love; with you I am well pleased."
Luke 3:21–22 niv

FOR THE SCARS

*J*esus, we long for comfort, and You are our comforter. We long for peace, and You destroyed the dividing wall of hostility. We long for wisdom, and You are the very Word of God spoken to us. We long for rest, and You are the Good Shepherd who leads us beside still waters.

But in our longing for these good things, let us not forget what else You promise to us. You promise we will have trouble in the world. You promise trials, tribulation, and temptation. You promise wars, famine, and earthquakes. If You didn't make it through Your time on earth unscathed, what makes us think we have the right to step into heaven free of scars from this life? We will be scarred too—despised, abandoned, beaten, mocked, and unjustly accused. We may be hungry and thirsty. We may have to carry more than we thought we could bear for longer than we thought we could bear it. But, praise God, that is not the end of our story, because it's not the end of Your story. You love us so much that You allow us to become like You in Your suffering. Help us to carry on, Lord, knowing that You are walking with us into glory. Amen.

"I have told you all this so that you may have peace in me. Here on earth you will have many trials and sorrows. But take heart, because I have overcome the world."
JOHN 16:33 NLT

Read Through the Bible in a Year

1-Jan	Gen. 1-2	Matt. 1	Ps. 1
2-Jan	Gen. 3-4	Matt. 2	Ps. 2
3-Jan	Gen. 5-7	Matt. 3	Ps. 3
4-Jan	Gen. 8-10	Matt. 4	Ps. 4
5-Jan	Gen. 11-13	Matt. 5:1-20	Ps. 5
6-Jan	Gen. 14-16	Matt. 5:21-48	Ps. 6
7-Jan	Gen. 17-18	Matt. 6:1-18	Ps. 7
8-Jan	Gen. 19-20	Matt. 6:19-34	Ps. 8
9-Jan	Gen. 21-23	Matt. 7:1-11	Ps. 9:1-8
10-Jan	Gen. 24	Matt. 7:12-29	Ps. 9:9-20
11-Jan	Gen. 25-26	Matt. 8:1-17	Ps. 10:1-11
12-Jan	Gen. 27:1-28:9	Matt. 8:18-34	Ps. 10:12-18
13-Jan	Gen. 28:10-29:35	Matt. 9	Ps. 11
14-Jan	Gen. 30:1-31:21	Matt. 10:1-15	Ps. 12
15-Jan	Gen. 31:22-32:21	Matt. 10:16-36	Ps. 13
16-Jan	Gen. 32:22-34:31	Matt. 10:37-11:6	Ps. 14
17-Jan	Gen. 35-36	Matt. 11:7-24	Ps. 15
18-Jan	Gen. 37-38	Matt. 11:25-30	Ps. 16
19-Jan	Gen. 39-40	Matt. 12:1-29	Ps. 17
20-Jan	Gen. 41	Matt. 12:30-50	Ps. 18:1-15
21-Jan	Gen. 42-43	Matt. 13:1-9	Ps. 18:16-29
22-Jan	Gen. 44-45	Matt. 13:10-23	Ps. 18:30-50
23-Jan	Gen. 46:1-47:26	Matt. 13:24-43	Ps. 19
24-Jan	Gen. 47:27-49:28	Matt. 13:44-58	Ps. 20
25-Jan	Gen. 49:29-Exod. 1:22	Matt. 14	Ps. 21
26-Jan	Exod. 2-3	Matt. 15:1-28	Ps. 22:1-21
27-Jan	Exod. 4:1-5:21	Matt. 15:29-16:12	Ps. 22:22-31
28-Jan	Exod. 5:22-7:24	Matt. 16:13-28	Ps. 23
29-Jan	Exod. 7:25-9:35	Matt. 17:1-9	Ps. 24
30-Jan	Exod. 10-11	Matt. 17:10-27	Ps. 25
31-Jan	Exod. 12	Matt. 18:1-20	Ps. 26
1-Feb	Exod. 13-14	Matt. 18:21-35	Ps. 27
2-Feb	Exod. 15-16	Matt. 19:1-15	Ps. 28
3-Feb	Exod. 17-19	Matt. 19:16-30	Ps. 29
4-Feb	Exod. 20-21	Matt. 20:1-19	Ps. 30
5-Feb	Exod. 22-23	Matt. 20:20-34	Ps. 31:1-8
6-Feb	Exod. 24-25	Matt. 21:1-27	Ps. 31:9-18
7-Feb	Exod 26-27	Matt. 21:28-46	Ps. 31:19-24

8-Feb	Exod. 28	Matt. 22	Ps. 32
9-Feb	Exod. 29	Matt. 23:1-36	Ps. 33:1-12
10-Feb	Exod. 30-31	Matt. 23:37-24:28	Ps. 33:13-22
11-Feb	Exod. 32-33	Matt. 24:29-51	Ps. 34:1-7
12-Feb	Exod. 34:1-35:29	Matt. 25:1-13	Ps. 34:8-22
13-Feb	Exod. 35:30-37:29	Matt. 25:14-30	Ps. 35:1-8
14-Feb	Exod. 38-39	Matt. 25:31-46	Ps. 35:9-17
15-Feb	Exod. 40	Matt. 26:1-35	Ps. 35:18-28
16-Feb	Lev. 1-3	Matt. 26:36-68	Ps. 36:1-6
17-Feb	Lev. 4:1-5:13	Matt. 26:69-27:26	Ps. 36:7-12
18-Feb	Lev. 5:14 -7:21	Matt. 27:27-50	Ps. 37:1-6
19-Feb	Lev. 7:22-8:36	Matt. 27:51-66	Ps. 37:7-26
20-Feb	Lev. 9-10	Matt. 28	Ps. 37:27-40
21-Feb	Lev. 11-12	Mark 1:1-28	Ps. 38
22-Feb	Lev. 13	Mark 1:29-39	Ps. 39
23-Feb	Lev. 14	Mark 1:40-2:12	Ps. 40:1-8
24-Feb	Lev. 15	Mark 2:13-3:35	Ps. 40:9-17
25-Feb	Lev. 16-17	Mark 4:1-20	Ps. 41:1-4
26-Feb	Lev. 18-19	Mark 4:21-41	Ps. 41:5-13
27-Feb	Lev. 20	Mark 5	Ps. 42-43
28-Feb	Lev. 21-22	Mark 6:1-13	Ps. 44
1-Mar	Lev. 23-24	Mark 6:14-29	Ps. 45:1-5
2-Mar	Lev. 25	Mark 6:30-56	Ps. 45:6-12
3-Mar	Lev. 26	Mark 7	Ps. 45:13-17
4-Mar	Lev. 27	Mark 8	Ps. 46
5-Mar	Num. 1-2	Mark 9:1-13	Ps. 47
6-Mar	Num. 3	Mark 9:14-50	Ps. 48:1-8
7-Mar	Num. 4	Mark 10:1-34	Ps. 48:9-14
8-Mar	Num. 5:1-6:21	Mark 10:35-52	Ps. 49:1-9
9-Mar	Num. 6:22-7:47	Mark 11	Ps. 49:10-20
10-Mar	Num. 7:48-8:4	Mark 12:1-27	Ps. 50:1-15
11-Mar	Num. 8:5-9:23	Mark 12:28-44	Ps. 50:16-23
12-Mar	Num. 10-11	Mark 13:1-8	Ps. 51:1-9
13-Mar	Num. 12-13	Mark 13:9-37	Ps. 51:10-19
14-Mar	Num. 14	Mark 14:1-31	Ps. 52
15-Mar	Num. 15	Mark 14:32-72	Ps. 53
16-Mar	Num. 16	Mark 15:1-32	Ps. 54
17-Mar	Num. 17-18	Mark 15:33-47	Ps. 55
18-Mar	Num. 19-20	Mark 16	Ps. 56:1-7
19-Mar	Num. 21:1-22:20	Luke 1:1-25	Ps. 56:8-13
20-Mar	Num. 22:21-23:30	Luke 1:26-56	Ps. 57
21-Mar	Num. 24-25	Luke 1:57-2:20	Ps. 58

22-Mar	Num. 26:1-27:11	Luke 2:21-38	Ps. 59:1-8
23-Mar	Num. 27:12-29:11	Luke 2:39-52	Ps. 59:9-17
24-Mar	Num. 29:12-30:16	Luke 3	Ps. 60:1-5
25-Mar	Num. 31	Luke 4	Ps. 60:6-12
26-Mar	Num. 32-33	Luke 5:1-16	Ps. 61
27-Mar	Num. 34-36	Luke 5:17-32	Ps. 62:1-6
28-Mar	Deut. 1:1-2:25	Luke 5:33-6:11	Ps. 62:7-12
29-Mar	Deut. 2:26-4:14	Luke 6:12-35	Ps. 63:1-5
30-Mar	Deut. 4:15-5:22	Luke 6:36-49	Ps. 63:6-11
31-Mar	Deut. 5:23-7:26	Luke 7:1-17	Ps. 64:1-5
1-Apr	Deut. 8-9	Luke 7:18-35	Ps. 64:6-10
2-Apr	Deut. 10-11	Luke 7:36-8:3	Ps. 65:1-8
3-Apr	Deut. 12-13	Luke 8:4-21	Ps. 65:9-13
4-Apr	Deut. 14:1-16:8	Luke 8:22-39	Ps. 66:1-7
5-Apr	Deut. 16:9-18:22	Luke 8:40-56	Ps. 66:8-15
6-Apr	Deut. 19:1-21:9	Luke 9:1-22	Ps. 66:16-20
7-Apr	Deut. 21:10-23:8	Luke 9:23-42	Ps. 67
8-Apr	Deut. 23:9-25:19	Luke 9:43-62	Ps. 68:1-6
9-Apr	Deut. 26:1-28:14	Luke 10:1-20	Ps. 68:7-14
10-Apr	Deut. 28:15-68	Luke 10:21-37	Ps. 68:15-19
11-Apr	Deut. 29-30	Luke 10:38-11:23	Ps. 68:20-27
12-Apr	Deut. 31:1-32:22	Luke 11:24-36	Ps. 68:28-35
13-Apr	Deut. 32:23-33:29	Luke 11:37-54	Ps. 69:1-9
14-Apr	Deut. 34-Josh. 2	Luke 12:1-15	Ps. 69:10-17
15-Apr	Josh. 3:1-5:12	Luke 12:16-40	Ps. 69:18-28
16-Apr	Josh. 5:13-7:26	Luke 12:41-48	Ps. 69:29-36
17-Apr	Josh. 8-9	Luke 12:49-59	Ps. 70
18-Apr	Josh. 10:1-11:15	Luke 13:1-21	Ps. 71:1-6
19-Apr	Josh. 11:16-13:33	Luke 13:22-35	Ps. 71:7-16
20-Apr	Josh. 14-16	Luke 14:1-15	Ps. 71:17-21
21-Apr	Josh. 17:1-19:16	Luke 14:16-35	Ps. 71:22-24
22-Apr	Josh. 19:17-21:42	Luke 15:1-10	Ps. 72:1-11
23-Apr	Josh. 21:43-22:34	Luke 15:11-32	Ps. 72:12-20
24-Apr	Josh. 23-24	Luke 16:1-18	Ps. 73:1-9
25-Apr	Judg. 1-2	Luke 16:19-17:10	Ps. 73:10-20
26-Apr	Judg. 3-4	Luke 17:11-37	Ps. 73:21-28
27-Apr	Judg. 5:1-6:24	Luke 18:1-17	Ps. 74:1-3
28-Apr	Judg. 6:25-7:25	Luke 18:18-43	Ps. 74:4-11
29-Apr	Judg. 8:1-9:23	Luke 19:1-28	Ps. 74:12-17
30-Apr	Judg. 9:24-10:18	Luke 19:29-48	Ps. 74:18-23
1-May	Judg. 11:1-12:7	Luke 20:1-26	Ps. 75:1-7
2-May	Judg. 12:8-14:20	Luke 20:27-47	Ps. 75:8-10

25-Jul	2 Chron. 13-15	Acts 22:17-23:11	Ps. 110:4-7
26-Jul	2 Chron. 16-17	Acts 23:12-24:21	Ps. 111
27-Jul	2 Chron. 18-19	Acts 24:22-25:12	Ps. 112
28-Jul	2 Chron. 20-21	Acts 25:13-27	Ps. 113
29-Jul	2 Chron. 22-23	Acts 26	Ps. 114
30-Jul	2 Chron. 24:1-25:16	Acts 27:1-20	Ps. 115:1-10
31-Jul	2 Chron. 25:17-27:9	Acts 27:21-28:6	Ps. 115:11-18
1-Aug	2 Chron. 28:1-29:19	Acts 28:7-31	Ps. 116:1-5
2-Aug	2 Chron. 29:20-30:27	Rom. 1:1-17	Ps. 116:6-19
3-Aug	2 Chron. 31-32	Rom. 1:18-32	Ps. 117
4-Aug	2 Chron. 33:1-34:7	Rom. 2	Ps. 118:1-18
5-Aug	2 Chron. 34:8-35:19	Rom. 3:1-26	Ps. 118:19-23
6-Aug	2 Chron. 35:20-36:23	Rom. 3:27-4:25	Ps. 118:24-29
7-Aug	Ezra 1-3	Rom. 5	Ps. 119:1-8
8-Aug	Ezra 4-5	Rom. 6:1-7:6	Ps. 119:9-16
9-Aug	Ezra 6:1-7:26	Rom. 7:7-25	Ps. 119:17-32
10-Aug	Ezra 7:27-9:4	Rom. 8:1-27	Ps. 119:33-40
11-Aug	Ezra 9:5-10:44	Rom. 8:28-39	Ps. 119:41-64
12-Aug	Neh. 1:1-3:16	Rom. 9:1-18	Ps. 119:65-72
13-Aug	Neh. 3:17-5:13	Rom. 9:19-33	Ps. 119:73-80
14-Aug	Neh. 5:14-7:73	Rom. 10:1-13	Ps. 119:81-88
15-Aug	Neh. 8:1-9:5	Rom. 10:14-11:24	Ps. 119:89-104
16-Aug	Neh. 9:6-10:27	Rom. 11:25-12:8	Ps. 119:105-120
17-Aug	Neh. 10:28-12:26	Rom. 12:9-13:7	Ps. 119:121-128
18-Aug	Neh. 12:27-13:31	Rom. 13:8-14:12	Ps. 119:129-136
19-Aug	Esther 1:1-2:18	Rom. 14:13-15:13	Ps. 119:137-152
20-Aug	Esther 2:19-5:14	Rom. 15:14-21	Ps. 119:153-168
21-Aug	Esther. 6-8	Rom. 15:22-33	Ps. 119:169-176
22-Aug	Esther 9-10	Rom. 16	Ps. 120-122
23-Aug	Job 1-3	1 Cor. 1:1-25	Ps. 123
24-Aug	Job 4-6	1 Cor. 1:26-2:16	Ps. 124-125
25-Aug	Job 7-9	1 Cor. 3	Ps. 126-127
26-Aug	Job 10-13	1 Cor. 4:1-13	Ps. 128-129
27-Aug	Job 14-16	1 Cor. 4:14-5:13	Ps. 130
28-Aug	Job 17-20	1 Cor. 6	Ps. 131
29-Aug	Job 21-23	1 Cor. 7:1-16	Ps. 132
30-Aug	Job 24-27	1 Cor. 7:17-40	Ps. 133-134
31-Aug	Job 28-30	1 Cor. 8	Ps. 135
1-Sep	Job 31-33	1 Cor. 9:1-18	Ps. 136:1-9
2-Sep	Job 34-36	1 Cor. 9:19-10:13	Ps. 136:10-26

ABOUT THE AUTHOR

Laura Freudig is a wife and mother of six who desperately needs to pray these prayers—and others like them—every day. She lives on an island along the Maine coast and fills her days with gardening, hiking, homeschooling, reading, and singing.